SUCCESS
FROM THE
HEART

D1306470

SUCCESS
FROM THE
HEART

PRESENTED BY

ADAM MARKEL
New Peaks

Presented by: Adam Markel

Producer: Ruby Yeh

Editorial Director: AJ Harper

Print Management: Book Lab

Page Design & Typesetting: Chinook Design, Inc.

ISBN-13: 978-0-9891792-5-6
ISBN-10: 0-98-917925-7

Printed in the United States of America

Contents

CONTENTS

CONTENTS

Adam Markel

INTRODUCTION

W hen I asked the thirty-five authors who created this book to trust that they had everything it took to be an author and that their stories were worth telling, most, if not all, had some doubts that this was true for them. Some said, "How can I be an author? What would I say that would be meaningful to someone else?" Others asked, "Would my story be useful? Is there wisdom in my experience?"

My response was simple: "Your heart is the key to having a more fruitful life. Listen to it," I told them. "Be quiet and present and listen. In this stillness you will see that you can experience a life that is bigger than the one you are currently living. You can inspire and change lives with your story."

One by one, they said, "Yes."

Success from the Heart is the book that will inspire *you* to say "yes." *Yes* to your deepest, most authentic desires. *Yes* to engaging in fulfilling those desires. *Yes* to living the life you were destined to live.

For our second book authored by New Peaks students, I chose the theme of heart-centered transformation because I truly believe that, whether we are aware of it or not, whether we acknowledge it or not and whether we believe it or not, our journey here on earth is a journey of the heart. I experienced this when I made the decision to follow *my* heart and leave my successful law career to devote myself to my own personal growth and to training others committed to personal growth as part of the New Peaks (formerly Peak Potentials, the largest personal growth training company in the world) team.

I have also had the unique privilege of witnessing first-hand the heart-centered transformation of tens of thousands of people over the past seven years. I watch the people who come to our programs and retreats first gain some awareness, then some understanding

---

***Our journey here on earth is a
journey of the heart.***

---

and then some empowerment to make lasting positive changes to their lives. It's the empowerment and connection that thrill me—when they finally trust and make decisions from the heart and have faith that their hearts will not lead them astray. Every day I get to see people taking action and saying *yes*!

When you follow your heart you are following the will of Source, of Great Spirit, of the Universe. When you deny your heart, you deny Source, you deny Great Spirit, you deny the will of God—you deny your destiny. When people deny their hearts' calling, is it any wonder that they have dis-ease or lack in their lives in some way?

I like to use the garden hose analogy. It takes a lot of energy to move water from one place to another. When you're standing on the garden hose, it is much more difficult for water to flow from one place to the next. Sometimes the water will merely be a trickle, and at some point it will stop flowing altogether. This is what happens when you are not connected to your heart and making decisions *from* the heart. The heart is your connection to the source of all creativity and wisdom, your connection to destiny and to your own divinity. The sooner you are aware of it and use it, the sooner that energy will flow easily and the sooner you will gain the results you seek.

If you are having trouble following your heart, remember that the mere fact that you are conscious of this means you are better off than most people, who aren't even aware that their heart is speaking to them. You are steps ahead of where you think you are. Slow down. Start with conscious breathing. In concentrating on your breath you will be come more present. The more present you are, the easier it will be to hear your heart. Feel your heart energetically: in the sensations in your body, in your feelings, in the thoughts and ideas coming up for you in the stillness. In my experience, these sensations, thoughts and feelings will lead toward inclinations to do something.

Remember, the head has questions and the heart has answers. You need both your mind and your heart, but your heart is "the

---

You are steps ahead of where you think you are.

---

doer." The heart is the part of you that says, "I want to ask my love to marry me." Your heart is the part of you that says, "I want to make a difference in the world." Your heart is the part of you that says, "I need to break from this person (or this job, or this friendship)." Your heart is the part of you that implores you to say *yes*—*yes* to long-held dreams, *yes* to possibilities, *yes* to contribution, *yes* to fulfilling your destiny.

These authors have created wonderful results in their professional and personal lives, and each one of their journeys began with listening to the quiet whisper of the heart. I am so proud of their process and their accomplishments. They are kin to me. They are my brothers and sisters—not just because they are New Peaks students, but also because they are life-long learners, committed to their constant and never-ending growth.

I've lived by the value of personal growth for more than ten years. It's one of the five ingredients to my own formula for successful results: intention, tenacity, rituals, constant and never-ending self-improvement (CNSI) and team.

In the pages of this book you'll see evidence that, in their own way, all of the authors used most or all of the ingredients of my formula to transform their lives. They also used it to create this book. They set an intention to courageously tell their heart stories; they were tenacious in their approaches to completing the book;

Allow the words to sit with you
so they can stay with you.

---

they followed their own rituals to find the truth in their spirits and to tell honest, brave tales to benefit you, the reader; they learned new skills and pushed themselves to grow beyond their comfort zones; and they worked as a team, collaborating to present you with this most precious offering: a book that will speak directly to *your* heart.

This is why implore you to approach this book differently. Recall that I said it is in stillness that we hear the heart and recall that ritual is one of the five ingredients for achieving successful results. With that in mind, I challenge you to take five minutes after you complete each chapter to sit in a quiet space and allow the inspiring words you've read to *land*. Allow the words to sit with you so they can *stay* with you. And then ask yourself… Am I ready to say yes?

Are you ready to listen to *your* heart, to take your foot off the garden hose and let the energy flow? Are you ready to find a deeper understanding? Are you ready to engage with your heart's deepest desires? Are you ready to make decisions *from the heart,* to take action *from the heart,* to succeed *from the heart*?

Yes.

Adam Markel is the CEO of New Peaks (formerly Peak Potentials), and the author of the forthcoming book Pivot *(Simon & Schuster – 2016). An international training firm, New Peaks has delivered world-class educational programs to more than one million people in more than one hundred countries.*

Before becoming CEO, Adam was the senior trainer with Peak Potentials and has personally trained more than a hundred thousand people in the United States, Southeast Asia, Canada, Europe and Australia. In addition, Adam is a keynote speaker for groups and conferences around the world including: Infusionsoft, American Gemologists Society, California Chiropractors Association, National Achievers Congress and Get Motivated. A recognized expert in the integration of business and personal transformation, Adam has been interviewed by Fox News, Newsday, The New York Post *and* The Wall Street Journal.

Before his work with New Peaks, Adam spent two years teaching junior high school English, founded a successful commercial real estate investment firm and went to law school—and passed the bar on his first attempt. After law school, Adam founded a multi-million dollar law firm specializing in finance, commercial and employment litigation. Over the course of his seventeen-year practice, Adam represented more than a thousand matters with hundreds of clients including Citybank, Wachovia and HSBC.

Adam holds a law degree from Saint John's University and an undergraduate degree in English from the University of Massachusetts Amherst, where he graduated magna cum laude. He passed the New York state, New Jersey state and Federal Court bar.

He lives in Carlsbad, California where one of his greatest joys has been raising four amazing children with his wife Randi. Connect with Adam at www.NewPeaks.com and www.AdamMarkel.com.

James F. Truesdale

A Defining Moment

Our most important decisions are not always made in response to grand, milestone moments. Our most important decisions are often made in response to moments that end before they begin. The defining moments, the moments that wake us up and implore us to change, to turn, to transform something essential about our lives; *these* moments happen in a flash. My defining moment occurred almost thirty years ago when I had a gun pointed at the temple of my head.

It was the summer after my freshman year at Rutgers University. I was visiting home and one afternoon decided to visit with some childhood friends. I had felt somewhat guilty about making it out of the hood when so many of my friends had not, and I wanted to connect and remind them—and myself—where I came from.

I am the youngest of seven children. I was raised primarily in Jersey City, New Jersey, which in the 1980s was known mainly for the ravaging effects that both crack cocaine and AIDS had on the community. Those were challenging times to live in the inner city; it was make-it or break-it for many teenagers. To my dismay, many did not make it. I did.

We had been hanging in the hallway of my friend's building, laughing and catching up, when two police officers burst through the door. It happened so fast. One moment I was standing in the foyer and the next I was up against the wall with the young officer's gun pointed at my head. I had no idea what was happening or why. *Had I done something that made the officer perceive me as a threat?*

My heart raced. I could die in a matter of seconds. I felt powerless and unprotected. *Who was going to save me from the police?* I was scared and I was angry. In that moment I knew: Life is precious and it could all end in an instant.

In the next moments it became clear to me that I had been mistaken for a person who had committed a snatch-and-grab robbery a block away. I did not fit the description of this person, but still, there I was anyway, one sudden movement from possible

---

I had a gun pointed at the temple of my head.

---

death. I felt sweat drip down the back of my neck and my muscles tightened. *How would I get out of this situation?*

Somehow, I had the presence of mind to calmly ask the officer, "Is it necessary to point a gun at my head?"

"Yes," he said. "I do not know what you have, so I am going to make certain you understand what I have."

I realized he thought I might have a weapon, which was preposterous to me. Still, in that moment I could see that he seemed concerned for his life. He was really afraid just as I was really afraid. Just as I was, he was afraid of dying, of losing his life before it began. I felt our connection. We were two young men standing off in a hallway, both with hearts racing, both terrified of what would happen next. When I realized he was just as afraid as I was, I believed I would be okay. At that moment, I knew for sure I had to create an environment where I could increase my value and preserve my life.

Fortunately for me, the individual they were looking for had been spotted, and it had become clear that I was not who they assumed I was. The police officer lowered his gun, and they left in pursuit of the person who did commit the crime. There was no apology. Some would say I was in the wrong place at the wrong time. But was my hometown the wrong place for me to be? Didn't I deserve to be there, to peacefully exist in my own neighborhood?

As my heart rate settled down and my breathing returned to normal, I could feel the shift in my bones: I would never be the same. I thought, *If it's going to be, it is up to me.* I couldn't rely on the world to embrace me, celebrate me or even perceive me as who I really am. I had to do that for myself.

As I walked home, I realized that many young people who looked like me would be subjected to the treatment I received from the police officer while in that environment. The environment was conducive to that type of fear-based behavior, where a police office fears for his or her life simply because of the color of someone's

---

I had to create an environment where I could increase my value and preserve my life.

---

skin. I knew I had to get out if I was going to have an opportunity to have an impact, be an example that there is a better way to live. I had to dedicate myself to my education, to working hard, to making something of myself.

After the event, a weight lifted. The guilt I felt about getting out of my neighborhood and leaving friends behind was replaced by my newfound determination. The event was confirmation that I was headed in the right direction. While I wouldn't want to relive that experience, it was the terrifying flash of a moment I needed to make real and lasting change.

Fortunately, I was blessed with a great brain, street wit, athleticism and a hard work ethic which afforded me the opportunity to complete my degree at Rutgers and my graduate studies at Carnegie Mellon by age twenty-four. Some educators called me "gifted and talented," but I viewed it as luck meeting preparation. Luck favors those who are prepared to meet the challenges of life.

In college, I began to realize that the magic ingredients for my success would be fueled by a simple combination: the Bible in one hand and a good book in the other, a dose of prayer and lots of focused actions. As I matured, I learned the importance of making proper decisions. I learned the importance of taking the necessary actions to move out of my comfort zone in order to pursue a more promising life. I began to understand the principle of sowing and reaping. Sow a good seed, reap a good harvest.

Anger is the enemy of reason. I could have directed my anger toward the police officer who had held a gun to my head, and my frustration with the reality of my situation in that neighborhood would have let it fester and grow into a destructive force. But another wrong does not make a right, and that choice would have been wrong *for me,* and for all I hoped and planned to be. And so

---

Sow a good seed, reap a good harvest.

I separated myself from the event. I let the moment of realization drive me forward toward success, but I did not attach myself to what happened. That became a moment of transformation *for me.*

In these turbulent and disturbing times, with *almost* every day a new person killed due to police brutality, it's important to remember that those moments often happen in seconds, seconds in which decisions are made—wrong or right—that are deeply personal for everyone concerned. I learned that, whether or not the people around you follow suit, you must maintain personal integrity at all times. I am not justifying the police officer's approach—or any police officer in any situation—but at that crucial, life-or-death moment all those years ago, I felt our connectedness as human beings. Perhaps, *from his point of view,* he was as much a victim of the environment as I was.

We all have defining moments that happen in the blink of an eye. What was your moment? When did you start to see things differently? What day did you realize life was not as it seemed, or that you needed to make a change? Your moment may not have been as dramatic as mine; it may not have been life or death. Think back on your life. When did you know things could be different, that they *had* to be different?

Today, it is quite evident that God was in the works that summer day. And, without a doubt, I was "preserved for higher things." Now I ask you, *how* did your moment change you? Mine gave me some experience of how the world might view me, which motivated me to think about how I *wanted* the world to define me, and how I wanted to define myself. The power in defining moments is in letting these moments of sudden revelation move us to take action.

If you haven't yet taken action on any of your defining moments, don't give up. You still can act. Those moments are yours; they are not lost to you.

Your present circumstances are not an indication of your future existence; but rather of your present thinking. The vision you have for your life is more important than any present challenge. The life you desire is on the other side of fear. Move in the direction of your heart's desire. Push forward even when no one seems to understand or appreciate your journey. If you have a strong will, a way will be made.

James Truesdale is managing partner and founder of OnTarget Consulting Services, LLC (OTCS), providing the best in project management consulting and project management training services in health, government, higher education and bio-energy. James is responsible for the overall leadership and vision for the current and future operations of the firm. He maintains the culture, vision and overall direction for the organization and its related entities. James serves as the public representative and spokesperson for the organization and is ultimately accountable for all actions of OTCS.

James earned a Bachelor of Arts in English and Africana studies from Rutgers University in 1989 and a Master's of Science, public management and policy, with a concentration in management of information technology, from Carnegie Mellon University in 1991. An author and speaker, James is currently developing the Entrepreneurial Institute of Servant Leadership and writing a book about his life and career, If Me, Why Not You? Connect with James at www. OnTargetConsulting.biz.

Danna J. Olivo

No Fear

I saw the headlamp of the bus before it hit me.

One moment I was happily crossing a crowded street in Rio de Janeiro enjoying the success of the day, and the very next moment a fast-moving bus was on top of me. In the space between the two seconds that seemed to stretch as if time could bend and shape itself to the experience, I realized there was no way I could escape the inevitable. I couldn't go forward or backward to avoid the bus. A sense of calm washed over me, and in a fraction of a second I made the decision to let go. In that moment, I was ready to die.

The fear I should have had gave way to acceptance and peace. They say that's what saved my life. Because my body was limp as a rag doll, when the bus made impact it threw me instead of slamming into me. Had my body remained rigid in fear, the bus would have run right over me, and I surely would have died.

Although I remained awake, I have no memory of the accident or being loaded into the ambulance until I became aware of the pain in my arm and in my ribs; it hurt to breathe. I was in a dreamlike state, confused and overcome with thoughts that somehow I had done this to myself.

The trauma unit at the intake hospital was dilapidated, filthy and overflowing with people. I was placed in a room with ten other people, no privacy. Surrounded by unfamiliar faces speaking a language I could barely understand, I received comfort and intent from their expressions and touch. My brain flooded with thoughts about my husband David, who was back home in the States. *Who would contact him? How would he handle the news? Would I ever see him again? Would I see my children, grandchildren? Who would continue my work in Brazil? Was this the end?*

As a business growth strategist and international business development consultant, I had been traveling back and forth to Brazil for the past three years, working to create inroads and find opportunities for United States businesses seeking to break into the Brazilian market. Before this period, I had never traveled internationally for business, but I saw an opportunity for my

---

In that moment, I was ready to die.

---

clients to break into the Brazilian market to take advantage of opportunities made available through the upcoming FIFA soccer world cup and the Olympic games, and I was willing to take a risk.

Things were going smoothly, and we were creating inroads to decision makers for my clients. We had finally reached a point of satisfaction and achievement, and now a bus had interrupted our plans—and possibly ripped everything apart.

As strangers busily attended to my injuries speaking a language I barely understood, I tried to push down fears: *Would I contract a disease in this hospital? What was happening to my body? What would happen to my business? Were all of our efforts lost?*

When I was informed that I would need surgery immediately to insert a tube into my left side, I resisted. The unsanitary conditions in the trauma unit made me fearful of the cleanliness of the operating room. I feared I would end up in worse shape than when I came in.

The intern said, "We need to drain the fluid from your lung and repair the damage to your head. If you do not have the surgery now you will die."

I agreed and came out of the surgery with forty stitches in my head and a tube that would stick out of my side for five days.

Fortunately, within forty-eight hours my international team was able to pull strings to get me transferred to a private hospital. There I learned the full extent of the damage to my body: seven broken ribs, a collapsed lung, lacerated liver, crushed right forearm, two blown eyes sockets, a hematoma to my left forehead and torn ligaments in my left knee. I knew I would not be leaving Brazil anytime soon. I feared I would never be the same.

In the weeks that followed, I went through a rollercoaster of emotions as I tried to overcome the physical challenges I experienced after the accident. I would stay in Brazil for almost two months because of my punctured lung. My husband was forced to leave me in Brazil after two weeks to return to work. Through surgery after surgery, I tried to maintain a positive mindset and persevere, determined to get my pre-accident life back.

It wasn't always easy to stay in this mindset. I remember a particularly low moment, when I first allowed myself to look in the mirror. It was two weeks after my accident when I finally allowed myself to face the damage done to my face. Seeing my bruised face and the stitches on my head was a total shock. It was worse than I

I was determined to face my fears and turn this bad situation into a positive learning experience.

imagined—the physical representation of a traumatic experience I perceived to be my fault. I broke down and could not stop crying for quite some time.

Still, I was determined to face my fears and turn this bad situation into a positive learning experience. Though I was nervous about returning to work, I wanted to get back on track with my business and our plans in Brazil, which had come to a screeching halt because I was the main driver of what was happening on the international front. During my recovery time in Brazil, I held court in my makeshift apartment with clients coming to me. All were sympathetic and accommodating.

After five surgeries and countless hours of rehab, I still felt some anxiety about getting back to my daily routine, but I couldn't understand why. With the help of professionals, I realized that I was suffering from PTSD on top of the physical issues. I had never considered the emotional trauma because I was so focused on my physical healing.

I needed to overcome these issues if I was to be completely whole again. I had always prided myself on the fact that I could overcome any challenge, but these emotional fears literally kicked

Fear is inevitable. What determines success is what you do *with fear.*

my butt. I discovered that I had refused to relive the accident in my mind lest it bring back the pain and fear that I had managed to block out. I did not want to do that. I did not want to relive any second of that experience.

I worked with a success coach to help me face my fears and deal with the emotional consequences of the accident. Allowing myself to remember those terrifying seconds before the bus hit me was a gift, because I recalled the feeling of peace and calm, of letting go and accepting my fate. That split-second mental shift had saved my life, and it would save it again. If I could face my fear and stop resisting the emotions that were holding me back, I could get my life back. I could get back to a *better* life, made richer by my experience.

Once I realized that I had to relive what happened to me to get past it, it was easier to get back into the game. Now I am able to use these lessons to motivate others. Today I realize that many obstacles in my personal and business life are only in my mind. I can break free of whatever debilitating thoughts or physical barriers are holding me back with the right determination and foresight. By examining what is holding me back and determining what I need to do to turn things around, I can take control and get around those obstacles.

Though I suffered many physical injuries, they were only obstacles. With the right mindset and motivation, I could still move forward. I realized that my physical limitations were only able to hold me back if I let them. The injuries, though extensive and painful, were much easier to overcome than the emotional fear of having to relive the accident and the fear of failure as a result of the accident. Now when I'm struggling with the emotional side, I try to uncover what is driving the emotions so I can ultimately defuse the fear and take some positive action.

My fears kept me isolated and restricted after the accident. What I have learned is, I had to accept the fact that I don't know all of the answers. Before, when I knew I didn't know the answers I always did my best to find them. What I've learned now is, rather than keeping myself isolated, I can save time, energy and frustration by reaching out and asking for help. First though, I had to accept the fact that I didn't know all the answers, and this is ok!

Today, I apply what I've learned from my accident in my work with clients. My strategic programs are all based around "lessons learned." These are lessons I've learned over my lifetime and I share these with my clients so that they don't struggle through the same roadblocks I have, so they go into them with open eyes, understanding there will be roadblocks, but these can be overcome. They may not be able to avoid the metaphorical bus coming toward them, but they can put plans in place to mitigate the fears that throw up the roadblocks. We can examine the "what ifs" driving our fears and then ask, "What am I going to do when I run into a roadblock?"

It's critical to realize that engaging in fearful thoughts and discussion about the possibility of roadblocks *brings* those roadblocks to you. If you were able to let fear go by believing in your true capabilities, things would run much more smoothly. If we could just eliminate fear and believe in ourselves, we would encounter fewer roadblocks.

Things happen in life, but it is up to you to decide if they will become roadblocks or steppingstones to better your life. Fear is inevitable. What determines success is what you *do* with fear. You can use fear as a tool for growth and let it guide the next step or you can let it beat you into submission. The choice is yours.

Danna J. Olivo is a speaker, business strategist and CEO of DAVNA Enterprises, LLC., a full-service business growth solutions company. Her passion is working with small and startup entrepreneurs to ensure that they start out on the right foot and stay on the path to financial freedom. With more than thirty-five years' experience in strategic planning with an emphasis on marketing and business development, Danna understands the intricacies involved in starting and running a successful business. Her efforts extend beyond the initial strategic planning process into the implementation and monitoring phase. As an intricate component ingrained into her client's business structure, she works diligently to keep her clients' accountable and on track to fulfilling their success goals.

In 2014 DAVNA Enterprises launched the Entrepreneur Prosperity Enrichment Program (EPEP), an educational program targeting small and startup businesses designed to educate and coach small businesses through the planning stage for their businesses. EPEP accomplishes this through webinars, workshops, one-on-one coaching, mentoring and strategic partnering programs.

A graduate of the University of Central Florida's College of Business, Danna holds degrees in both marketing and management information systems. She has extensive experience in strategic marketing and business development within the architectural, construction, engineering and transportation markets working for both large and small firms locally and internationally.

Danna is currently working on a new book, Going for Gold: The Entrepreneur's Guide to Owning Your Fears and Breaking Through the Barriers of Mediocrity. *Connect with Danna at www.DannaOlivo. com. Danna also publishes a bimonthly newsletter chock full of tips and tools for small and emerging businesses. You can sign up by sending an email to bpsnewsletter@davna.com.*

Leonard Huffman

CROSSING THE FINISH LINE

Seminars saved my life—but only when I was ready. Most people attend personal and professional development seminars looking for a pathway to a better life. Some come looking for miracles. Almost everyone leaves inspired and charged. Hardly anyone actually acts on what they learned. And yet they go to still more seminars, searching for answers.

I was no different. For years I attended seminar after seminar. Most were very educational, but not many really helped me at the time. I learned a lot, but I always had a reason why it didn't apply to me, or I immediately had my own twist that would make it better. My twist usually didn't make my plan better; it made it fail.

Finally, in late 2013, I had the thought: *If it works for everyone else, why not for me?*

The obvious answer was: *Maybe I'm the problem.*

I'm a Marine. That's where I got over hating to run and learned to love it. In 1990 while in training in Quantico, Virginia, I was ordered to help support the Marine Corps Marathon in Washington, D.C. I spent six hours on a Sunday filling and handing cups of water to people who were running the marathon. My water station was at about mile 23, near Haines Point. I was very hung over, and thought the runners were crazy.

I was also moved at how people late in the day kept going. The winner crossed the line at roughly two hours, twenty-five minutes. But four hours later people were still running, walking and staggering by on their way to the finish line. I began to realize that marathons aren't just about winning. They are about proving something. The realization stayed with me, but if you would have asked me that day if I would ever run a marathon, I would have said, "No way. It seems impossible for a guy like me." My weight had always been an issue for me, and I hated running.

I graduated from my MOS school in Quantico, and was sent to Okinawa, by way of home for two weeks over Christmas. Two weeks of eating Polish food with my grandmother telling me, "You're too skinny!" was not helpful. I lost a lot of weight just to get into bootcamp, now I was reporting in at Okinawa ten pounds overweight.

Marines are unforgiving about tight uniforms. I was given two weeks to get myself back into shape, or be forced to join a special work-out platoon and be babysat at meals. *No freaking way was I going to let that happen.* I all but quit eating and started to run

---

*I learned a lot, but I always had a
reason why it didn't apply to me.*

---

every day. I got the weight off fast, in less than a week. Strangely, I had a mind shift. Running stopped being something I had to do. It became something that helped me. I began to relish my running time. Just me, my thoughts, improving physical fitness test (PFT) scores, and nobody but me caring about what I ate.

In May of 1991, I was sent to Saudi Arabia as part of Desert Storm. I'm no war hero. While the actual fighting was happening, I was washing dishes on Okinawa. (Showing up for duty overweight gets you the crappiest details they can find.) In Arabia, we worked twelve-hour days every day. In the evenings there wasn't much to do. Read, watch forty-year-old movies at the common movie screen, lift weights or run. The movies sucked. The weight room was always packed and gross—think Saudi heat in August. I read more than fifty books while I was there. I also ran, a lot.

The Gunny whom I reported to was an incredibly fit man. He noticed how I ran to relieve boredom. He was a marathoner. He got me to join a group of distance runners. Those runs were much longer than my daily three to five miles. I had a blast and, from then on, I was hooked on distance running.

I'm a little different than really good natural distance runners. I have short legs and my family tree is very plump on both sides. The really good distance guys are very long-legged and rail thin. I have

---

I could barely move and every part of my life was in turmoil.

---

to take about fourteen strides for every ten the natural runners do. When they run, their feet barely hit the ground. When I run, the impact is like a sledge hammer. I have broken the running board on my treadmill three times. Almost any problem or feeling could be either solved, or the solution would be thought of while running.

We left Saudi Arabia in October of 1991. My next duty station was 8th & I, Marine Barracks, Washington, D.C. On my way to D.C. I had a two-week layover at home. Again at Christmas. Again my grandmother telling me I'm too skinny. Again, I was given two weeks to get my crap straight. I did. Again by running, and barely eating. This time I had some really cool stuff to look at. The area around 8th & I was basically a war zone, but get three blocks away, toward the Capitol, and it's freaking awesome.

Three years before, I was hung over, amazed and wondering why anybody would run a marathon. Now I not only knew why, I signed up to run it too. A buddy of mine ran it with me. As we crossed the half-way marker, the winners' times were announced. We didn't care. We kept going and finished. Neither of us could walk well or trust our knees for two days. We did it!

The following spring my enlistment was up. I left the Marine Corps and D.C. I took a really good job in Iowa. I was no longer in a runner's paradise, but I kept on running for my health and the mental clarity it gave me.

Then, in 1997 I went to the doctor to find out why my joints hurt so much. I thought he'd tell me I was overdoing it. Instead he said, "In ten years, you won't be able to walk without an aid." I was diagnosed with psoriatic arthritis. It was a crushing blow. The world as I knew it was dying.

"He's a quack," I told myself at the time. Then, I pushed on, as Marines do. My knees and feet got worse, but I went on to run two more marathons in 1999 and 2000. Then it wasn't just my knees

I wasn't following the systems I learned.

and feet—my hips, shoulders, ankles, elbows and wrists got worse, too. I ran one more marathon in 2002. By 2003, I couldn't run three miles. By 2005, I couldn't run my own driveway.

Over the next eight years my joints got progressively worse. Some days I needed painkillers just to get out of bed. More times than I can remember I spent weeks using stairs one step at a time, because a knee had flared and couldn't be bent or trusted to support me. I had to replace my car because it was a stick. I couldn't count on being able to use both arms and legs to drive.

At various times I tried many different drugs and treatments. Some worked for a while, and then started causing side effects worse than the condition they treated. I spent thousands on prescriptions a year. I gave myself shots in the stomach and legs. In 2007 I said, "Enough." I stopped taking everything. Sure my joints hurt like hell, but the drugs were destroying my liver and making me feel like crap. From then on it was only over-the-counter painkillers, and only when the pain was too much to take.

During this time I realized, *I'm not running, so I have an extra hour and a half free each day. How should I spend my time? I want to make more money, but I'm really limited on what I can do.*

When I refinanced my home in 2006, the broker said, "With your credit, you could make a fortune in real estate." I checked it out and bought a house to fix and flip. Bought another one. After the market crashed, I decided to educate myself about real estate. I read books. Went to meetings. Then I started attending seminars. I haven't had a vacation of over two days in the last six years that wasn't spent at a seminar. I've gone when I had a fat wallet, and when I wasn't really sure I should go because things were very tight. I've been to seminars all over the country.

Almost every guru I've read recommends reading T. Harv Eker's *Secrets of the Millionaire Mind*. I was skeptical, but read it. It made some sense, but seemed a little voodooish to me. They offered a free seminar, The Millionaire Mind Intensive (MMI), halfway to my mom's house in Detroit. *Why not try it out? I can do the seminar, then go see Mom.*

After five years of attending seminars with little or no results, I was not expecting much.

The seminar saved my life. By the time I went to the MMI, I was in my own personal hell. I had lost a lot of money in real estate. I had legal battles. My dad had a heart attack and my uncle died. There were constant problems in my job. The stress made my joints flare like the fourth of July. Something every day. Often more than

---

You pay for your education one way or another.

---

once a day. I could barely move, and every part of my life was in turmoil. A knot formed in my gut. Things eventually stabilized, except I was traumatized. I kept doing my normal things, but now almost anything unexpected sent my mind into dark places. When my phone rang and I wasn't expecting a call, my reaction was dread. *Now what? Is Dad ok? Is there a problem at work? Who's sick?* The knot in my gut was as normal now as the aches in my joints. Always there, nothing I could do about it.

After three long intense days at the seminar, lots of hugging and grown men in tears, I noticed the knot was gone. Not fading, just gone. That realization was better than sex. I literally jumped for joy. With my joints, it wasn't much of a jump. Luckily, at that seminar, it happens all the time, so nobody noticed. Suddenly my mind was free. All those seminars I'd taken that I thought just didn't apply to me made sense.

It took me five years to actually hear something that I heard in every pitch: "… if you follow the system…"

I wasn't following the systems I learned. All the real estate training now made sense. I actually started making money at it. Most importantly, at a real estate bootcamp a year before, I had heard Terry Givens give a presentation called "The Healthy Body Reset." It was all about getting younger as you age, ridding your body of toxins, and eating healthy. When I saw him my mind was full of *I know this* and *I'm already seeing several doctors,* so I barely listened.

After the MMI, I felt empowered, and my most urgent need was to fix my body. I remembered Terry's presentation. I went to his website, and rather than put my own twist on his system, I actually did what he said. Within months, I was walking without pain. By July of 2014, I was able to run a mile! I had to stop because my leg muscles got tired, not because of my joints screaming in pain. You probably cannot understand how happy I was to have sore leg muscles. It darn near brought a tear to my eye.

I am now running two miles nonstop, then mixing walking and running for another mile and a half three days a week. I'm not cured, but I am functioning much better. The good days are now the norm. I still have flares, but those are the exception, not my everyday experience. Recovering from a flare has gone from weeks to two days or less.

You pay for your education one way or another—whether it's in an academic setting, or books, or seminars and workshops or through expensive mistakes. But you won't get the most out of whatever you're learning if you don't get your head right so you can listen and take action. A seminar is useless if you do nothing with the information you learned. And a seminar is a waste of time and money if you never should have gone in the first place.

I've been to dozens of seminars. I can tell a good seminar from a mediocre seminar. I can tell you what works and what doesn't, who has great content and who doesn't. In fact, I built a website so people in search of pathways to success can evaluate the merits of various seminars based on reviews of past attendees. Ultimately, you've got to spend your energy and money learning how to do what you actually want to do. Don't get sidetracked on the other stuff. Ask yourself, "Is this something I need to learn how to do, or is this something I'd be better off paying someone else to do?"

Seminars inspire, educate and ignite passion in attendees. Seminars can change your life—maybe even save it. But if you're not ready, seminars are a waste of time and money. Fulfilling a dream, healing your body, earning a fortune—these are goals that may seem as impossible as running a marathon seemed to me all those years ago. But if you attend the right seminar, the *best* seminar for your needs, and then listen with an open mind and open heart, you'll have the steps and tools to get where you want to go. Baby steps. Walk. Run. Blocks. Miles. Soon enough, you'll cross the finish line.

Leonard Huffman is the founder of Seminar Traveler, a website dedicated to helping people get the most out of personal and professional development seminars for the least expense of time and money. While serving in the United States Marine Corps (USMC), he participated in Desert Storm, met three presidents, visited Camp David and participated in the 1993 presidential inauguration. After leaving the USMC, Leonard earned a degree in business from Mount Mercy College in Iowa and began a career in computer programming. After attending dozens of seminars, he developed the first website for seminar reviews. He is the author of The Seminar Traveler. *Connect with Leonard at www.SeminarTraveler.com.*

Fredly Antosh

It's About Love

I am in the love business.

I started in the matchmaking industry shortly after I first came to Southern California seventeen years ago. I was having a hard time getting past the Hollywood facade that is so prevalent here to find quality people to date. I thought, *I'm super-outgoing and I can talk to anybody, anywhere. If* I'm *having a hard time finding quality dating prospects, I can only imagine what happens when someone more reserved is trying to find someone.*

Many matchmaking companies prey on people when they are lonely. Lying and misrepresentation is commonplace in the industry. From the beginning, I intended my company to be different. We won't overpromise and we tell the truth. Above all, we advocate connection on a heart level. In every aspect of business— whether I was finding a good match for a client, working with my team or speaking and training about relationships—for me it has always been important to come from the heart. We are all the same: Eeveryone wants love.

That I value love first and foremost has helped me build a successful business. In my experience, if you operate business from a love perspective, the money will come. Marianne Williamson calls this the Law of Divine Compensation. She explains, "To whatever extent your mind is aligned with love, you will receive divine compensation for any lack in your material existence. From spiritual substance will come material manifestation. This is not just a theory; it is a fact. It is a law by which the universe operates."

For me, there was never any other way to approach life. I still remember so clearly thinking at a very young age, *Love is the meaning of life.* By the age of five I knew in my heart that love is all that matters and that we come to this planet to learn about love. I couldn't understand why everyone else didn't know that. People around me were caught up in accumulating money and gaining status, and I knew that would not fulfill my purpose here on this beautiful blue marble.

Later in life I learned that, when people come back from near death experiences, they report that their lives were reviewed not for their accomplishments, but rather for how well they loved and how willing they were to *learn* to love, how they demonstrated love

Love is the most powerful energy on the planet.

and the opportunities they took to love *more.* People who have had near-death experiences almost always say, "Love is all that matters." My mission in life is to learn to love better. Since that is my mission, is it any surprise I'm in the love business?

I knew from an early age that I came to this planet to be an example of love, peace and harmony. Growing up with a lot of abuse in my childhood has blessed me with the ability to intuitively know and feel other people's pain. Being tender hearted, empathetic, patient and loving has helped me care for others, especially in matters of the heart.

The essential teachings I provide to my clients, and to audiences for which I speak, apply not only to finding a romantic partner, but also to every aspect of life. This is because finding a good match begins with exploring your past and identifying the patterns you unconsciously duplicate.

When we are unconsciously controlled by our family histories, we make the same bad choices over and over again. We choose partners who make our lives difficult. We walk toward the familiar, repeatedly choosing the same negative outcome, even when our hearts cry out for a different result, a different reality. Most people will not take the road less traveled, one that involves self-reflection, brutal honesty and a willingness to find love at any cost.

The Science of Love

After seventeen years of interviewing people and analyzing thousands of relationships, I am confident in my estimation that ninety-eight percent of us duplicate old bad patterns in relationships. We go from one relationship to another, picking the same type of partner over and over. The two percent who don't duplicate old bad patterns usually flip-flop from one extreme to another. With nearly two decades of data and statistics about how people choose partners at my fingertips, it is easy for me to predict what type of person someone will choose. Normally people are not aware that they are stuck in a pattern until I point it out to them.

People are drawn to the familiar, even if that pattern isn't healthy for them. Most people do not believe they are stuck in a pattern. If someone makes a blanket statement such as "all men cheat," or "all women are crazy," or "all men want is sex," or "all women care about is money," that person is stuck in a pattern.

Being stuck in a pattern just means you have blinders on because of your past experiences. My job is to show you something completely different to get you out of that rut, to open you up to a whole new world. I help people identify their bad patterns and then introduce them to a different type of person, essentially breaking their patterns.

One of the most important factors in determining if someone would be a good partner (in heterosexual relationships) is if they had a loving and respectful opposite-sex parent. If they did, they will have an easier time establishing and maintaining a good relationship. However, all bets are off if they choose a partner who came from a lot of drama and chaos. Primary relationships set a precedent for all other relationships thereafter. What we see, we duplicate. For example, if a woman had an abusive alcoholic father, chances are she will have trust issues with men. No matter how trustworthy a man may be, eventually she will see her father in him. If a man had a difficult relationship with his mother, he is likely to have a hard time maintaining relationships with women.

What people see between their parents growing up is what they believe is normal and true, and they will often end up in situations very much like their parents'. For example, if their parents always fight, the child/adult either fights with their significant other,

---

You have to be aware of
connections from the past.

---

or chooses to not engage in intimate relationships because they appear to be too difficult. Of course, usually there is a lot of push/ pull as most people want closeness and love. All too soon, the remembrance of the pain of fighting resurfaces and then they have to get away from the relationship.

I'm not suggesting we all have to have perfect parents in order to find love. However, be aware that if we choose partners who have issues with their opposite-sex parent, we should not expect those relationships to be easy. If you think about the most successful, effortless relationships you've had, it's likely your former partner had a good relationship with an opposite-sex parent.

The science of love is about finding a winning combination in a partner for the best possible outcome:

1) Their opposite-sex parent was loving and respectful, or, if that was not the case, the prospective partner is willing to work on their issues with this parent in therapy or through other personal growth opportunities.

2) They have seen a functional relationship with at least one of their parents.

If a prospective partner does not have a winning combination, all is not lost—as long as the other partner has a strong family background, so someone can guide the relationship in a positive way. That partner can "set the rudder" for the other partner, and if that person is wiling to follow their partner's lead about conflict resolution, loving with respect and the give-and-take in a relationship, it could work out beautifully. These are all learned behaviors and if they aren't learned from your parents, then they can be learned in an intimate relationship.

When you are making a transformation, you have to be aware of connections from the past. The past can only control us if we are not aware of the effect on the present, and then aren't willing to make a different choice. When they see that they have been in the same pattern year after year, most people desperately want to make a change. However, being aware is only half the battle, because awareness does not automatically influence attraction and chemistry. We are still attracted to the same type of people and still have chemistry with the same type of people. This is why it's useful to have help in choosing a different partner.

How many times have you seen a friend who just keeps picking the same type of person over and over? You could pick better for them than they do! There is a good way to break those patterns: Let

*My mission in life is
to learn to love better.*

someone else do the picking, because they won't have your pattern and they will have perspective and distance from the situation.

When Glen came to us for help, he was sick and tired of being sick and tired. He had spent his adult life as a superhero of sorts, saving pretty, busty blondes from near disaster. Like a hummingbird, Glen was attracted to the sweet nectar of the "train wreck." The women he chose to date had had troubled childhoods, financial problems, daddy issues and addictions. Divorced three times, he was worn out and wondered if true love with a mature woman was in the cards.

In a Skype call from New Orleans Glen said, "I need you to set me straight and introduce me to a centered, mature, pretty woman, because I can't trust myself to do the picking."

We introduced Glen to six women, each of whom would be a good match for him, and, after spending more time with two of them, he hit it off with Victoria. Six months later, they are having a ball, traveling the world and enjoying life—with *no* drama.

Over the years, hundreds of people have told me I need to write a book about this topic because they found the information I shared with them so helpful. Some of my clients have said, "I learned more going trough this process with you than I learned in ten years of therapy." I started working on my book, *The Science of Love*, in earnest this year because I know that many people would benefit from learning the simple truths about finding a good match. In writing this book, I am fulfilling my childhood promise to become a divine messenger of love.

I have found that the love business is the most interesting business to be in, because people are so fascinating. I can assure you—life is much stranger than fiction. Nobody would believe the stories I've heard from my clients!

I sign off every email signature with the phrase, "It's about love." I believe love is the most powerful energy on the planet. I believe this because love is all that matters. Before he passed away, I had the good fortune to see Dr. Wayne Dyer in person. He was a shining example of living a life of love; in his last years he was often seen wearing a sweatshirt that simply said: "love."

When I was in high school I had every word of John Lennon's song "Imagine" written on my folder. I still hope that he was right, and that I am not alone in my Pollyanna world where we live in peace and love. Just imagine what a magnificent world it would be if everyone tried to love better, every single day.

Fredly Antosh is recognized nationwide as the matchmaking guru for affluent men. As CEO of The Dating Source, she has worked in the world of upscale matchmaking for seventeen years. She has been the director of sales, has been heavily involved in recruitment and works closely with matchmakers to meet the toughest standards of clients throughout the United States, Canada and Europe.

Widely quoted in press releases, Fredly has worked with the best in the world of high-end executive dating. Partnering with authors, relationship coaches, recruiters and matchmakers, Fredly creates dynamic content about love and successful partnerships. She is currently writing a book about her secrets and strategies for finding your best match, The Science of Love. *Connect with Fredly at www. TheDatingSource.com.*

Dr. Nicole Erna Mae Francis-Cotton

BELIEVE IN YOURSELF
AND PRESS ON

"Dear Lord, if it is your will for me to stay…"

A year after graduating with honors from Oral Roberts University with a Master's degree in marriage and family therapy, I visited the island of St. Martin in the Caribbean for vacation. Having grown up in St. Martin, I wanted to spend some time there before returning to the United States to assist my cousin Dr. Aldansa Ambrose in his ministry.

As I explored the island I saw that the once vibrant youth movement on St. Martin had become stagnant. Many young people—mostly young boys and men—were sitting on corners being idle, despondent and depressed.

My heart bled as I observed the deteriorating condition of the lives of these young people.

In a time of prayer, I sought guidance from God as to what my role was in changing this trend. I prayed, "Dear Lord, if it is your will for me to stay on St. Martin and serve the Caribbean region, then close the doors for me to return to the United States."

So asked, so done, and the rest is history. With not a cent to my name, not knowing how my mission would be realized, I set forth on a path to see the youth of my nation transformed, restored and enlightened. I wanted to reconcile individuals, couples, families, the church, governments and nations to our Creator and each other, demonstrating that we can live victoriously by the living word of God. And so, the Victorious Living Foundation (VLF) was born.

Despite my deep faith and conviction, soon after starting the vision for VLF with my supportive family members, I recognized the financial resources to maintain and sustain the vision were waning, as the government and other entities seemed unable to see the significance of investing substantially in preventive programs to propel our youth forward.

I set forth on a path to see the youth of my nation transformed.

I told potential donors, "People are hurting. Our community is fragmented. Young people are frustrated. Marriages are failing and families are falling apart. Juvenile delinquency, crime and violence are increasing. We need hope and tools for creating lasting and positive change. We need restoration."

When doors would not open, when people of influence would not heed our call, I remembered the source of my strength and all that I needed was God to sustain us and the vision. The significance of my faith in God through Christ is important to share, considering the girl I once was.

At age eight, my family and I migrated from Antigua to St. Martin. Homesick for the land of my birth, I struggled with anxiety, poor self-esteem, culture shock and other internal struggles as I tried to adjust to our new home. An introvert, I shied away from people; I focused on my studies and graduated from high school at the age of sixteen.

At the age of seventeen I enrolled at the University of Tampa in the honors program. Despite my previous accomplishments, including being a popular reporter for the local St. Martin newspaper, *Newsday,* I was still very shy with low self-esteem. I kept asking myself, "Why are you part of the honors program? You're not smart enough."

It was then that I learned the truth of Proverb 23:7 that states: "As a man thinks in his heart, so is he."

By the end of the first semester, I became one of a handful of honors students to make the Dean's list, which I made every semester until I graduated, as well as the National Dean's List every year.

Recalling this turning point moment in my life, I decided I would not allow myself to become the victim of circumstance. I would not be defeated. I relied on my faith in God and the fact that the vision I was running with was not my own, but was divinely imparted—therefore, the vision *had* to succeed. I would forge on, no matter what obstacles appeared in my path and no matter how hopeless it seemed.

I drew upon my inner resources and reflected on the birth of the vision and received guidance as to how to move forward. I enrolled in various Peak Potential programs and other empowerment

---

**VLF has made an impact on the
lives of thousands of people.**

---

initiatives that expanded my network and my net worth, and continued to press forward with the re-birth of the vision.

Since its inception in 2002, VLF has made an impact on the lives of thousands of people. More than one hundred individuals, families and marriages have been restored or strengthened. Through our mentorship program, more than one hundred youth have avoided juvenile delinquency and crime, have stayed in school and improved their grades and their self worth. Thousands of youth and young adults have been empowered through our Gospel concerts; conferences such as Xtreme Youth Fest, *Wealth Creation Series;* youth radio program, *Fresh,* which is an outreach radio program for youth by the youth of our youth wing, Y2X, which was established in 2003 to breathe fresh content into the airwaves; and other empowerment programs.

Many graduated at the top of their classes and became successful teachers, lawyers, graphic designers, certified public accountants, specialists in international business, professional athletes and entrepreneurs.

VLF provides food, clothing, emotional and spiritual support to the less fortunate. We visit and minister at the prison. We have seen young men who have been in the penal system change their lives around: gain and sustain employment or start their own businesses and stay out of the penal system through our programs. The young people on the corners, sitting idle with nothing to do? We connected with them and enrolled several in leadership and other trainings.

I am incredibly proud of the participants in our pilot Youth Entrepreneurship Program. In just one year we successfully assisted nine individuals in opening their own businesses: one sells jewelry; another became a caterer; one started a messenger

Tremendous power lies within you.

service; another provides in-home manicures and pedicures to her customers; three participants joined forces and opened a construction business; another runs her own taxi service; and one came directly from the block and with our help and the Lord's guidance, he lifted himself out of the street life and opened his own car wash with two other partners.

I know now that as long as I remain in faith and see every obstacle from the perspective of a victor and not a victim, and every stumbling block as a steppingstone, I will continue to thrive. I will continue to share the vision by persisting and not giving up, and eventually the greater vision will be realized. I am eternally grateful to my parents, Oswald and Kathleen Francis, my sister, other family members, friends, donors, board members, past employees, volunteers and well wishers who have believed in the vision of Victorious Living. Without them we would not have achieved as much as we have. I am also thankful for my husband, Roy Cotton, Jr., who is also running with the vision.

Tremendous power lies within you. There is a greater purpose in your life and a Creator who loves you and wants you to be reconciled to him to have a more fulfilling and rewarding existence. One person can truly make the difference. It matters not where you start, but how you finish.

If you are struggling in pursuit of that dream, acknowledge where you might be playing the victim role. Readjust your perspective and reframe your challenges as opportunities to overcome. Make a conscious decision to connect to your Creator and earnestly seek His heart for guidance and direction in your life. Take the necessary action to fulfill your dreams and visions that you have been placing on hold, for fear of failure or disbelief in yourself or your visions.

If you have a vision, a dream or plan close to your heart, believe in it. Believe in yourself. Press on! The mere fact that you have received this vision ensures that it will succeed. God would not give you a dream without the power, tools, resources and determination to realize it. "So ask and you'll receive. Seek and you'll find. Knock and the doors will be opened to you." (Matthew 7:7, in the Bible).

And so begin. "Dear Lord, if it is your will for me to…"

Believe In Yourself
Forging up your hill of strife,
you feel that you won't make it.
Then, like dawn breaking,
you see images on the other side
of your mountain.
Your spirits lift.
Your strength is revived
And you forge on.
Finally realizing that victory is nigh,
you breathe a sigh of relief.
You still stumble sometimes,

but alas you've made it to the other side.
You look behind you
at the distance you've travelled;
and wipe your brow in disbelief!
Disbelieving that you've made it.
Then your faith becomes strong;
and you look forward to the future.
Knowing now that you can overcome
anything and everything
that comes your way.
Because you believe in yourself!!
Believe in yourself!
Believe in yourself!
by Dr. Nicole Erna Mae Francis-Cotton
(Originally published in *It's Time for Change* and included
on her CD *Poetic Vibes to Help You Thrive*.)

Dr. Nicole Erna Mae Francis-Cotton is the visionary and President of Victorious Living Foundation (VLF), an organization dedicated to reconciling individuals, couples, families, communities, churches, governments and nations to our Creator and each other. Since its inception in 2002, VLF has had an impact on the lives of thousands of people through its innovative approach to personal and community development. She developed VLF's successful mentorship program, Victorious Living Family and Friends Network™, catering to youth between the ages of five and nineteen. The program's mission is to prevent juvenile delinquency by providing youth with positive role models, life empowerment skills, anger management, self-esteem building, tutoring and career guidance, as well as parenting skills and support for their parents.

Dr. Francis-Cotton is a transformational leader, certified success coach and a marriage and family therapist. Through her authentic and passionate love for life and people, she has helped persons of all ages, races and cultures, couples, families and organizations, to make positive and lasting change. She holds a BA in psychology from the University of Tampa, a Master's degree in marriage and family therapy from The Oral Roberts University, and an honorary doctorate of divinity from Grace Hill Bible University.

As an EFT practitioner, Dr. Francis-Cotton gets tangible and amazing results in helping clients to alleviate emotional and physical pain as well as overcome traumas, phobias and other challenging dilemmas. Certified in the Democratic Dialogue process through The United Nations Development Plan's (UNDP)'s Virtual School, she is also equipped to utilize dialogue as a tool to overcome problems, transform conflicts and empower social change.

Dr. Francis-Cotton is the author of It's Time for Change, *an anthology of her inspirational and motivational poetry, and* How to Thrive in Trying Times, *which presents a profound message of hope. She is also the producer/singer/poet of* Poetic Vibes to Help You Thrive, *a CD of her poems sung and recited to powerful and inspiring music.*

Dr. Francis-Cotton obtained her "Train the Trainer" certification with the renowned training company, Peak Potentials, which equips her to be even more effective as a trainer/leader. She is also an officially recognized and accomplished entrepreneur through the prestigious CEO Space business club.

To connect with Dr. Francis-Cotton and to learn more about the Victorious Living Foundation visit www.VictoriousLivingSXM.org.

Mong Sai

FIND YOUR NORTH STAR

One of my traditions is to send a holiday card to treasured friends and family each year. It's a small gesture to send my well wishes to those who have made my life a little happier because I know them. After receiving one of my cards, an old colleague, Gregg, whom I respect immensely, sent me a message that read: "Loved the card and your family. How are you?"

Those three simple words "How are you?" hit me like a ton of bricks. I knew he genuinely wanted to know. I was numb: immobilized and frozen in time. I couldn't lie about it even though I wanted to. I finally responded that life was not great. After several months of working with a trusted colleague on a business venture, I found myself swindled of my life's savings and going into debt. I needed to sell the home that my family and I lived in to pay off the debt; all two-hundred fifty-thousand dollars of it.

As a first-born Chinese American, I had saved this money by making many sacrifices to take care of my family and save for a "rainy day." In a blink of an eye, it was gone. I avoided interactions with everyone, including my husband and kids, so I could hide from my embarrassment and guilt. Those months were the darkest point in my life. I felt like an utter failure. I couldn't see any light and I could not find my purpose for living. I was lost. My spirit was broken. After all, how could someone "so smart" be so stupid? How could I let something like that happen to me, to my family?

I will never forget what Gregg wrote back to me to give me hope and confidence to fight back from this blow that struck me hard and left me dead inside. He shared that he too had had a business failure with a partner and it had taken him a few years to recover from it. I wasn't the only one to believe a partner and be duped.

Gregg said, "It'll be okay. This experience will make you a stronger and better person. Not today or tomorrow but *one* day.

I found myself swindled of my life's savings.

And when you look back on this experience, you will be thankful for what it taught you."

What Gregg said to me was my wakeup call. I needed to stop beating myself up. I wasn't the only one who had something like this happen to them. I needed to nurture my mind back to health, learn from what happened and bounce back. I finally got up from being beat down and chose to *live* again. I came close but I didn't permanently break!

Life will always throw you curve balls. Some will throw you off your game and cause you to step to the sideline. The most important thing is to regroup and get back in the game. Never give up!

Sometimes curve balls come at us at the onset of a new role. Most people are excited to start off. They dive in feet first, eager to learn the ropes. Typically, a new hire will receive some training on new systems and processes, spend time with their manager on expectations and priorities for their roles, and then it's off to the races. They are left to their own devices to figure out how to "make things happen." And yet very often, the information new employees are given is not sufficient to do their jobs effectively. They need to navigate the company waters and make sure they can stay afloat knowing who and what are their life-lines.

Does this sound familiar to you? Perhaps you started a new position ready to take on the world, and by the end of your first week felt frustrated and confused, unsure of how to achieve all that was expected of you—and sometimes not even sure *what* was expected of you. Your manager assumed you knew because you read the "job description" and you got hired for the job. You may have started having second thoughts about where you landed.

As an experienced employee, you may have struggled with different obstacles in your professional life: bosses who didn't provide you clarity or guidance to handle challenges when they surfaced; co-workers who resisted your recommendations to do the best thing for the company; feeling burned out from assuming additional responsibilities on top of an overflowing workload.

Life will always throw you curve balls.

Whatever the roadblock or issue, have you mentally checked yourself out of the game before it even started or ended or can you refocus on your purpose and devise a strategy using the tools and resources you possess to finish the game strong? After all, as they say, "It's not how you start but how you finish that counts."

So many reasons get in the way of reaching our goals at work, and they all seem perfectly reasonable when we tell ourselves the story to justify why we can't accomplish something. The task is too difficult. You failed the first time you tried. You're too busy to complete your project. You don't have enough know-how to see the project through. You don't have the fortitude to risk failure in front of peers and colleagues.

In the workplace, people often look to me to give them "a pass," to let them know it's okay that they didn't complete an assignment for a training class, or missed a meeting because they forgot. I always tell them, "I will never tell you it's okay not to do something. It has to be okay with *you*." Life is about choices and tradeoffs, and at the end of the day, you need to be okay with where you focus your energy.

Having coached many people through different issues, I have noticed when they are not performing at their full potential, it is because they are one or more of the following:

1. Unclear about their purpose.
2. Not one hundred percent committed to their work, thus bringing little or no energy to work.
3. Missing the courage to do or say something that is needed.
4. Unproductive with their time, letting distractions get the better of them.
5. Apprehensive to influence people—or themselves—to make things happen.

When you have clarity, energy, courage, productivity and influence in what you choose to focus on, with all these elements firing on all cylinders, you are invincible.

Success takes energy, initiative and a desire to succeed in spite of whatever situation is thrown your way. Sometimes we lose focus or forget the purpose of what we do. We get so lost in the motion of checking things off that to-do list that we don't remember the significance of our actions. We need to focus on keeping our head in the game. We need someone to be our north star, to remind us or help us clarify our purpose and then to act with intention toward achieving our goals.

Cracking the workplace success code is not difficult. There is a simple playbook to becoming a workplace superstar. Just as in any sport, there are rules on how to play and win. However, you do need to invest in preparation and be willing to develop excellence in these areas consistently. Therein lies the challenge. I'll share some of my best tips with you.

Master your mindset—When you walk into work, what aura do you present to your colleagues, your manager, your clients? Are you open to new ways of doing things? Are you optimistic, enthusiastic and positive? Do you consistently generate new and innovative ideas for your organization to consider?

Master your fundamentals—Be an expert in your craft. Take responsibility for excelling at your job skills and continuously staying abreast of knowledge in your industry, whether through formal education, self-directed learning or networking. Become known as the go-to person in your area of expertise.

Model the way—Demonstrate the behaviors of exemplary business professionalism, whether it is taking initiative where needed, being considerate of others or sharing your knowledge and expertise with those who can benefit from it. How do you willingly help others and foster synergies in the workplace?

Find a coach—Whether it is a good friend or a hired professional, a coach can help you see the blindspots you don't see in yourself—both areas for development and untapped talents—to help inspire and challenge you to do more, be more. Everyone needs someone to help them believe they can do it.

When we are at our best, we can inspire others to greater performance through the examples we set. And to me, that is pretty awesome. That satisfaction with sharing the best of your talents and doing meaningful work can be yours, too. Working with purpose fuels you more than any amount of money or title could;

Cracking the workplace success code is not difficult.

those are great things, but long-term do not keep you inspired. You will cultivate a relentlessness in dealing with roadblocks and a fundamental belief that the desired outcome will be achieved. Failure is simply not an option. Achieving your goals becomes a welcome challenge, and the journey to get there is all the more sweet as you work to fine-tune your success strategy.

Did you know it took Thomas Edison one thousand attempts before he invented the lightbulb? With your purpose at the forefront of your mind, you will discover that you are willing to do whatever is necessary to reach your goal. Can you remember a time when you were in the zone, excited about work and pleased with your performance? That feeling can also come from being part of a winning team, or being part of a big project creating something new or making something special happen. You can have that feeling consistently if you know what to focus on.

No matter what your situation: whether you are a new hire; have been working at the same company for ten years; have a great manager who develops and coaches you or an non-existent manager who could not care less about your personal development and growth; work at a large multi-national company where there are vast learning resources or a small mom and pop company—you can dictate your own breakthrough in your professional development by choosing to place time and effort on it.

Invest in making *you* stronger and better. Be willing to always do whatever it takes to succeed, even when others may say, "Why work so hard? Take a chill pill." They don't understand your purpose and they don't need to. Only you need to.

It's tempting to take the easy road, but life's sweeter when you have the scrapes and scars to show for your successes. Life is made of many moments. At any time, life can be wonderful, or it can be challenging. No matter where you are, make a commitment to make one shift for yourself. If life is great, can you recognize when someone else needs some words of encouragement and be their north star? If you're unsatisfied with the results in your life, what are you willing to do to make it better? The first step is always the hardest.

My north star Gregg reminded me what I knew but couldn't see. My message is that you are all one connection away from someone inspiring you, giving you the courage to get out of a rut or your comfort zone and fueling you to pursue those goals that make your heart sing. Don't be afraid to fail. It is part of the journey to success.

Mong Sai is a mentor, coach and trainer. In her twenty years of professional experience in the corporate learning and talent development industry, she has served in senior positions at Newegg, MetLife, American Express, JPMorganChase, and The Forum Corporation. Mong designs and develops experiential learning solutions that address practical business issues, provides high performance coaching to individuals and teams and facilitates training sessions, all with the goal of cultivating employee growth and development in their professional careers. She has worked with all levels of employees from frontline to C-level staff. Her mission is to share her life stories of successes and failures to inspire people to persevere toward achieving their dreams.

Mong graduated from NYU Stern School of Business with a BS degree, and went on to earn a Master's of distance education from the University of Maryland. She is a Certified High Performance Coach, and a Peak Potential Quantum Leap graduate. She enjoys spending quality time with her husband Jack and kids Jessica and Tyler, baking, hiking, cooking, playing SCRABBLE™ and volunteering in her local community. A first-generation Chinese American who speaks Cantonese and Hainanese, Mong is a native New Yorker currently residing in the Los Angeles area.

Mong is passionate about empowering individuals to be their ultimate best. She is currently writing a book about the life lessons she learned while coaching employees at work, The Workplace Playbook: 7 Winning Strategies for Superstar Success. *Connect with Mong at www.CoachMong.com and see how she can propel you or your organization to success.*

Elena Pezzini, PhD

Heart Rescue

Virtually everything you need to learn in life, you can learn from your pet.

As a psychologist and certified life and business coach, I have worked with Oscar-winning celebrities, Olympic athletes, bestselling authors, world-renowned speakers, Fortune 100 company's CEOs and entrepreneurs at every level of success, from startup to those running hundreds-of-million-dollar companies. Ninety-nine percent of the time, clients come to me because they want to make more money or want more time off or both. Discovering that they can achieve this by listening to and caring for an animal usually comes as a surprise.

It is the simplest ideas and the easiest paths that often seem hard to believe. And yet they are the surest way to success and fulfillment. Everything relates to everything, and so, everything is a reflection and extension of yourself. Money—having it or not having it—is a result of the thoughts and beliefs you hold inside of you, consciously or not. Animals are mirrors, reflecting to you your anxieties, fears, frustrations, concerns, joys and so on. Have you noticed that, when you are anxious, the animals around you are anxious? When you are calm, your animals are calm. Animals soak up the essence of who you are—your thoughts, beliefs, struggles and desires—and show you the truth of who you are in this very moment. I have noticed it, too. Humans are, by definition, animals. Now, if animals don't stress about money, why should we humans stress? Animals stay in the present moment and never stress about money, knowing and trusting they will always be okay.

I invite you to pay attention to the animals in your life. Are your pets happy? Playful? Do they follow their training? Or do they seem nervous or scared? Do they make messes in the house and generally cause trouble? Or, if you do not have pets, how do animals react to you when you encounter them? Are they over-

---

Animals see the real you.

---

excited, or calm and loving? In my opinion, how animals behave around you and relate to you gives you clues as to how you perceive yourself and how you are perceived by the world.

I have witnessed that, beyond the mirror, animals remind you who you *really* are, the person you are yearning to reconnect with, the person who, like so many abandoned animals on this earth, needs to be rescued. Animals see the real you, the child with eyes full of hope and a pure and positive heart. Our pets have kept their innocence. They know what matters most in life: unconditional love, healthy food, clean drinking water, plenty of exercise, restful sleep, constant companionship and abundant play. They remind you that this is the true, balanced path toward living a fulfilling life.

I am an immigrant. I came to the United States from Italy and made it on my own. It wasn't easy. Because I was so far from my family, my pets became my family. When I felt discouraged, my pets kept me balanced and helped me stay on track. I'm highly grateful for them.

Over the years, I have become more and more interested in how animals help us heal, help us grow, help us live happy and balanced lives. I began to study the human-animal bond and wrote my PhD dissertation on the subject, while helping my clients create the lives they desired. Today, I apply my knowledge about the healing and transformational power of animals to the work I already do with humans.

There are about eight main life areas—money, career, relationships, health, education, environment, play and charity—and your pets will help you succeed in all of them. Recall that I believe animals act as a mirror, and that they remind you of the child within you, the time when you made heart-centered choices. These benefits alone would be enough to motivate most people to pay special attention to their pets and all that pets can teach humans. And yet there is much more that animals have to give us.

Taking time to love, feed or exercise your pet, or with your pet, enables you to focus on one thing and one thing only: your relationship with your pet. When I am walking my dog, or just sitting with my cat and dog and giving them my attention, this is one of the few times I'm able to stop my mind from racing and feel pure bliss. When my clients are stressed, I always tell them

Pets love unconditionally.

to do some sort of art, or movement such as yoga or dance, or meditation with their pets.

Your pet also is fully one with you and does not leave you unattended or out of sight. I always smile when I am inside a store and have left my pet momentarily tied outside or in the car (with open windows) and I peek outside and I see those two eyes completely, one hundred percent hyper-focused on me. The world could come to an end and those eyes would still be on their human. The power of focus!

It is scientifically proven that animals aid in reducing and often eliminating stress. Pet owners live longer and are generally happier than non-pet-owners. In this way, animals help you improve all life areas. When you slow down and stay focused on one aspect of your life, then you are better able to make real and lasting positive change. Have you ever been able to remain sad when you look into an animal's eyes?

People who care for pets tend to be more grateful. They learn this from their pets. Animals have always shown people gratitude for feeding them, for saving them, for paying attention to them. They never hold back affection and constantly show appreciation. Can we say the same about our own actions, or about the humans

*What if you loved yourself as
your pet loves you?*

in our lives? I can't always say so. Gratitude is a key to success in all areas. And yet we often forget to express our thanks for the simple pleasures, such as for being alive.

Pets love unconditionally. They don't hold grudges. They love everyone—poor or rich. They don't care about material possessions. They live for their owner's affection. When I am with my pets, I feel nothing but unconditional love. I feel it from my animals to me, and I feel it toward my animals. In human relationships, unconditional love is hard to come by. Many people place conditions on love. They withhold love when they don't feel safe, or if they feel someone has not earned their devotion, or as punishment. Worse, they do it to *themselves.*

My pets taught me unconditional love and unconditional commitment. I had never experienced it before. Growing up in the countryside in the Lake Region of Northern Italy, I have fostered or adopted the animals nobody wanted. Born after the Chernobyl nuclear disaster, some of them were deformed. Although they didn't look like the ideal pets I had always dreamed of—the purebred, perfectly designed pets so many people want—inevitably, they won my heart and taught me the meaning of true love. In this way, they become ideal and perfect to me.

This is my life lesson: How many times do we want the perfect career, the perfect partner? And we wait and wait and don't take action. We let life slip away waiting for the illusion of perfection. From my pets I have learned that, if there is such a thing as perfection, it is in the journey. With all the surprises and unexpected turns, as long as we go for it and don't hold back, life will reward us beautifully for our courage and for taking action. That has been my beautiful experience.

What if you loved all humans as your pet loves you? What if you loved yourself as your pet loves you? How would your life be different if you loved without condition?

Again, animals remind us what is important: play, being present, love. Animals don't think about the future. They don't worry about tomorrow. They are happy for no reason! In our pursuit of success and money, we lose sight of the simple things and stop living. Most Western societies measure success with money. I am an international person with two passports, Italian and American. I have seen, met and befriended hundreds of thousands of people from all over the world. In my experience, some of the happiest and healthiest people are not the richest. I have met some unhealthy and lonely monetarily rich people. The happiest and healthiest people in my life take time to smell the roses, accept what is and continue loving themselves and other beings, no matter what! They are balanced, and I believe in balance.

At the start of this chapter, I said that ninety-nine percent of my clients come to me because they want to make more money. They come to me in a state of blaming anything and everyone except themselves. With coaching, they realize that they are solely responsible for their financial results and all their other life results and that when the other areas of their life are out of in balance, it prevents them from making more money. As they start working on themselves and open up to nature, to animals, to the child within them, they begin to know themselves better and make better decisions—decisions from the heart, from a loving place instead of from a place of darkness.

Again, how we relate to one thing is how we relate to everything. People who can't relate well to the most innocent creatures on Earth ought to look inside themselves and ask why. Why are they impatient? Why do they discriminate? Why are they angry? If people can't convey love, tranquility and peace to an animal, they certainly can't offer it to other humans.

In my life, the best lessons have come from nature. I have seen animals win the hearts of fearful people, negative people, and transform them for the better. Animals provide valuable lessons—for free! When you rescue a pet without a home or family—through foster or adoption—you rescue your own heart, you rescue yourself. Some animals can be vegetarian, which makes it very affordable to provide for them. Mine are! If you don't have a pet, or can't foster or rescue one for some reason, please visit and volunteer at an animal sanctuary. Spend time with animals and in nature. Why not let animals teach you what you need to learn? Then be ready to fall in love with all other beings and watch miracles happen!

Elena Pezzini, PhD, is the founder and CEO of You Have Got the Power, Inc. and You Got The Power, a 501c3 nonprofit, both coaching, consulting and mentoring organizations dedicated to empowering people and their animals to make the Earth a better place. At the core of the companies' vision is a commitment to make this world a better and better place to live in for ourselves and the many generations to come: homes for all people and animals, education, financial literacy, human rights for everyone in the world; and a clean, ecological, sustainable, organic and healthy Earth for all of us!

Guiding clients on five continents, Elena and her team use positive psychology, coaching, hypnosis, emotional freedom techniques, masterminding, mentoring, consulting and neuro-linguistic programming to help them achieve their wildest dreams and fullest potentials in life by facing and breaking through their fears. In her webinars, Elena shares the insight, tools and strategies she uses to help clients achieve remarkable results, often collaborating with popular coaches such as Lisa Nichols from The Secret*; renowned Internet marketer, Peng Joon; speaker Les Brown; bestselling authors Robert Kyosaki, Mark Victor Hansen, Jack Canfield and Dr. John Gray; various celebrities and NFL players.*

A native of Italy, Elena moved to the United States to pursue her PhD in industrial organizational psychology. She has worked as a coach and consultant for a number of Fortune 100 companies, including Procter & Gamble, Ernst & Young, Showtime, General Electric, Sprint, Prudential, Bank of America and Charles Schwab.

Elena is also certified in life, financial, leadership and Navigator Franchise coaching. She is a Senior Coach with her corporation, with her nonprofit and other world-leading companies in personal and professional education. Elena is a regular contributor to Business Heroine Magazine. *She is a member of the International Coaching Federation, the American Society of Training Development and the European Association of Work and Organizational Psychology. Connect with her and her team at www.YouHaveGotThePower.com.*

Fátima López

BUILD THE WORLD YOU WANT

You can't do that. Has anyone said that to you? Or, have you ever said that to yourself? Often, the people we love the most cut off our wings in order to protect us. More often, we cut off our own wings and choose not to fly. We decide to play small.

If someone had told me two years ago that I would create, with my father, the first eco-library in Mexico I would have said that he was nuts. We didn't have that big picture in mind at that time, but we did have the burning desire to share knowledge and consciousness wherever we could. It was an idea that, to some, seemed impossible. My heart knew differently.

Though I was brought up in a very poor environment in a *vecindad*, a tenement we shared with many other families, my parents handed down to us their common love for books and knowledge. My father, Pedro López, grew up in extreme poverty and struggled, studying and working at the same time so he could get an education and better his chances for a bright future. He was ambitious. He worked three jobs at a time so that his children could eat while he cultivated his obsession for knowledge reading everything that crossed his path.

I grew up surrounded by books; they were my toys, my best friends. My dad took us out from that neighborhood and eventually, his efforts paid off and, when I was granted admission to the prestigious Universidad Iberoamericana, he made it possible for me to go. My friends from childhood weren't that lucky. Some joined gangs while teenagers and got killed, eventually. Most of the girls got pregnant at around fifteen. Books and knowledge literally changed my timeline.

A little over two years ago, my father told me he wanted to make his collection of books (around forty-six thousand at the time) available to the people of Tepoztlán, a small, poor community near

It was an idea that, to some, seemed impossible.

Mexico City that had little or no access to books, or cinema or cultural experiences. As in many small towns in Mexico, when the children finish school for the day they have nothing to do. Violence is growing, because teenagers join small drug cartels, kidnapping groups and mafia groups. But what if they had somewhere to go? What if they had a library where they could read, and learn and discover new ideas about the world? What if they could see a different version of themselves through books and culture?

Working with my father on this project was a natural fit for me. I am a poet and published author. My first job in television was hosting a show about books and writers. Knowing firsthand the power of knowledge and art, together we began planning the project. Our primary goals were consciousness, education and sustainability—building an ecologically sustainable library. Ecological sustainability is near and dear to my heart. I wanted to create a building that was one hundred percent off the grid and honored nature's processes.

Our goals were ambitious, yes. But not impossible. Still, at every step of the way we encountered naysayers who said, "You can't do that," simply because it hadn't been done before. No one had ever built a sustainable library before.

We pushed forward with our project, consulting with architects, engineers and builders. We created spaces for patrons to read, to attend workshops, to hold meetings, to watch cinema and other cultural events. The sustainable component of the library was my passion. We installed solar panels, tried to re-use every material during the building period and did not see anything as waste. Since Tepoztlán is a warm place, the architect designed a thermic system to retain the heat in the roof and inject (through a fountain) fresh breeze into the building through the floor. We built containers for collecting rain water. We installed systems for limiting energy use.

For six months before the opening of the library, we asked for the federal government's recognition as a public library. The National Library Department said, "You can't do that."

"Why not?" we asked. The reply was one you may have heard in your own life: "Because nobody has ever done that before." It was the first time in my country that a person made his entire library available to a community. We knew we were pioneers and we wanted to open a path for any other person who wanted to donate their books to a community in the future. How would anyone know an idea is impossible until they try?

No challenge could take away my peace.

But, following my dreams hasn't always been natural to me, because I was told they were not right for me or for others. Though I had some success hosting a show on television some years ago, what I've always really wanted was to become an actress. Sometimes, to find true happiness, we have to destroy the life we have. We have to say "no" to others in order to say "yes" to ourselves. I came to realize, if I wanted to have the life of my dreams, I would have to build it for myself. Eventually, my heart lead me to break with the life that I was living and start over, but the immediate consequences were dire. One moment I was living in a beautiful apartment and the next I was standing on the street, completely broke, surrounded by two suitcases and ten boxes of books.

My friend Karina offered to let me stay at her place. My room was an unfinished laundry room, the size of a bathroom. I didn't have enough money to buy a mattress, so I slept on the floor. The bathroom was three floors down, in Karina's apartment. I had a new job at a publishing house to make ends meet and just enough money to pay for the bus until my first paycheck arrived. I knew I couldn't spend one peso on one other thing.

For three months, I cried every night. The room was often infested with bugs, the floor was hard and cold, and wet from water that leaked in, but still I carried on. I had a vision for the life I wanted and I knew the conditions I was living in were only temporary. I had followed my heart, and no challenge could take away my peace. I signed up for an acting class on weekends, the first shy step toward answering the call of my heart.

Over the years, and with the help of mentors, I continued to grow as an actress. At times I was scared to try out for roles, but I kept at it. I landed my first job, and then another. A student film here, a play there. Eventually, I started to make enough progress

---

My happiness is not negotiable,
and neither is yours.

---

with acting that I could focus most of my time on it. I was offered a role on a soap opera and then one in a play that had a long, successful run. I made my own rules, plotted my own course, followed the beat of my own heart, and it paid off.

I had made my own dream possible and I knew we could make my father's dream a reality, too. When opening day for the library finally came, we still hadn't heard from the government about our request. That morning, I went to the pool at my hotel, right at the base of El Tepozteco, a mountain which the ancient cultures considered sacred, and meditated in silence. I was completely calm and at peace, grateful for what we had achieved.

We had invited several people from the government, but we weren't sure if they would show up. When we were about to start the opening ceremony, two things surprised us. First, the Governor arrived with all the local Secretaries. We were so pleased! And then, a representative from the National Libraries Department came in. He handed Dad a document that certified our inclusion in the National Library System. We had made the impossible, possible.

That day, more than four hundred people enjoyed speeches, music and cultural presentations. I talked to many reporters. They were amazed. Some said, "Nobody but you and your father could have done this. Mexico needs more people like you."

This statement bothered me. People looked at us as heroes, but they couldn't see themselves as potential heroes, too. "Everybody can make a difference," I said over and over, "You don't have to build a physical building." I believe that. We didn't plan to found the first eco-library in Mexico; we just wanted to share our books because we knew knowledge can change lives. What we build within ourselves is more important. Love and integrity for our planet will manifest in small actions, and that's exactly what nature needs. Small, meaningful actions lead to big, profound changes.

At the library we give art workshops in painting, sculpting, theater and dancing, and have a book club. Almost two hundred children and teenagers attend the clubs after school. We have more than fifty thousand books, including three thousand children's books, and more than twenty-six hundred films and documentaries, a playground, a small movie theater, an acoustic stage for concerts. We have been open for a year, and have already made an impact on around ten thousand lives.

The other day we had an event focused on astronomy. We brought scientists from the National University in Mexico City. They came with telescopes and showed patrons how to observe the cosmos. It was a transforming event for them and for us. Standing there, watching young people look up at the sky—all of whom had never seen a close-up picture of the moon or the planets—I thought about the choices I made to get me to this moment. Every time I ignored my heart, it was a struggle. Every time I took a risk and ignored the people who said, "You can't do that," I succeeded.

As the children looked up at the stars, I thought about my own dream. My dream of being an actress realized, I am now working on breaking into the United States market. In the stars I see my own bright future. I saw it when I took my first tentative step and signed up for an acting class. I saw it when I lay my head down at night on a cold, wet floor and cried myself to sleep. It has always been there, this dream of mine, guiding me from the sky.

My happiness is not negotiable, and neither is yours. It doesn't matter how we are judged, or how much we don't fit in our environment or society; we are in this world to expand ourselves by making *us* happy. We are responsible for our own joy, which has a lot to do with being truthful to our dreams. The more we are our true selves without judgment, the more we live for our Higher, Divine Purpose and so, the more we contribute to the expansion of others. Are you living the dream of your life? Or are you living someone else's idea of happiness? Or have you given up on your dream, simply because someone told you, "You can't do that"?

You are the dreamer and you are the genie. You *can* do that brave, beautiful thing. Actually you *can*.

Fátima López is an actress, poet and bestselling author. For two years she was the host of Entrelíneas TV, *a television show about writers and books for Canal 22, a cultural channel in Mexico managed by the government. During this time she decided to follow her true passion and pursue an acting career, taking acting classes on nights and weekends. After performing in a few short films, Fátima appeared on* La impostora *and* Lo que callamos las mujeres, *collaborating at Argos for Telemundo as well as TV Azteca.*

The co-author of six published books, Fátima has also written her first poetry book, which will be released in 2016. With her father, Pedro López, she planned and successfully opened the first eco-library in Mexico, Centro Cultural Pedro López Elías (CCPLE), the first private library to become part of Mexico's National Library System and the second largest library in the State of Morelos. To donate to CCPLE, visit www.ccple.com. To connect with Fátima, visit www.FatimaNow.com.

Nancy Gaines

How to Escape

At age forty-eight I retired from the work world. It wasn't because I received an unexpected inheritance, won the lottery or cut back on Starbucks to save for my magic retirement number. It wasn't because I'd worked crazy hours since I opened up my first lemonade stand; I didn't even have a job offer when I completed my college undergrad years.

I was able to retire from the nine-to-five (or five-to nine) by consistently learning and taking the right financial actions one step at a time until I reached financial freedom. But it wasn't wealth or money freedom that drove me to succeed. It was fear—a fear born the year I turned sixteen.

It was the Tuesday after Labor Day. As I was leaving school the principal approached me and said, "May I drive you home?"

That's weird, I thought. She'd never offered to drive me home before. I said, "I can walk," since my house was just a few blocks away. Besides, I was a teenager; I didn't need an adult to escort me home. But she insisted, and I figured her driving me home was an order, not a request, so I followed her to her car.

When we arrived at my house there were several cars in the driveway: my mom's, my grandma's, a neighbor's and our priest's. Again I thought, *This is so weird. It's the middle of the afternoon. People should be at work.*

As I walked toward the front door, my younger brother opened it. "What's up?" I asked.

He said, "Dad died."

Two simple words and still I couldn't process what he was saying. Dad was on a business trip. Surely my brother was mistaken. Again I said, "What?"

"Dad died," my brother repeated. "He had a heart attack." Finally, it sunk in. *My dad was gone.*

Later, after the people left and it was just Mom's car in the driveway, I said to her, "Dad had life insurance, right? I'm sure we're going to be just fine with money. You took care of that for us, right?" I was worried. He'd left her to raise four kids alone, and she only had a small income from a part-time job.

My mom gave me a look I'll never forget—part guilt and part fear. She said, "We planned to buy a policy when Dad returned from his trip."

My mom gave me a look I'll never forget.

Even at my young age I knew that life insurance doesn't count unless it's in place before the death. Still, I didn't think much about our money situation after that; the shock of losing my father and the grief that followed was overwhelming and all-consuming.

Several weeks later, the sheriff pulled into our driveway. My mom came running down the stairs, gathered us kids together and in a stern whisper said, "I will punish you so hard if any of you answer the door or make a sound." She was shaking. I'd never seen her so scared, so despite growing up believing that the police were good, helpful people, I did what she said.

It wasn't until I was older that I realized why the sheriff had come to see us: We might lose our house due to nonpayment Mom's part-time income and the social security checks were not enough to pay the mortgage.

The day I learned we almost lost our house was the day I decided I would never be broke. *Never.* That decision carried me through years of education. I earned a Master's degree in business administration; I read many books on money, investing and business; I learned how to buy real estate, trade stock and invest in businesses. And I learned by doing—by making mistakes and implementing different strategies, I discovered how to ensure I would never be broke.

So often you hear people talk about the desire to become wealthy. It wasn't the end goal of wealth that drove me; it was the fear of losing everything. The unexpected side effect of my mission

> *I've been playing small and I want to do bigger things.*

to avoid going broke was I ended up building multiple streams of passive income. I truly scared myself into wealth!

It wasn't until I decided to play bigger that I realized I had unintentionally achieved a life of money freedom.

One day, while sitting in a personal development class, it hit me: My calling is to teach others how to build their own income streams and businesses so they can leave their jobs and follow their passions. I wanted everyone to have peace of mind and the freedom to spend their time following their dreams outside of a job. Then I realized: *There isn't enough time in a day to work at my job and start a company to help others.*

At the time, I was working as a senior managing consultant for IBM Global Business Services. I did some quick math in my head and confirmed that I earned enough passive income each month to replace my salary. The revenue streams I'd created in order to avoid homelessness were the key to following my calling. I didn't have to wait, or save up, or try to find investors. I could just break up with my job and follow my dream.

I've always advised my clients who want to transition out of the work world to prepare to talk to their partners about making the change, rather than spring it on them before they have worked out the answers to possible questions, or when they are still having insecurities about the decision. In my case, I figured out how I wanted to go about it, and then I brought it up to my husband, Jed.

"I decided to quit my job. I've been playing small and I want to do bigger things," I told him. "I've run the numbers. We have enough money to pay the mortgage—which is really our only debt. I've started other businesses before, and I know this will be successful as well. And if it doesn't work, I can always find another job."

Jed didn't even question me. He just smiled.

"I know I can do this," I said.

"I know you can, too. I'm not worried," he replied. Then, we picked a date for me to quit my job—about three months out.

Today, I help others quit their jobs with purpose to follow their dreams and launch amazing companies. With proven tools, insight and systems, I give them the advantage to succeed in their endeavors. Many speakers and coaches give lots of hope, but they don't give lots of how. I love guiding people in the how, providing

---

Dreams die when we don't plan and prepare.

---

them with actionable steps they can do right now to get where they want to be. Hope is not a strategy. You prepare financially to leave and determine what you want to do, and then I help you launch a business or dream with success. People can join me at any one of the steps depending on where they are in life.

One of my favorite client success stories is Stef. A successful computer engineer at a great company, Stef did not like her job. She didn't like going to work and thought it was incongruent with her calling: to help people live healthier lives. When we started working together, she had left her job in order to give her part-time personal training business her full attention.

Stef is amazing at training, but realized she had some gaps in business knowledge. She recognized the power of having a business consultant guide her through the startup phase versus doing it alone, which would take much longer. She had a good start, but we worked together to really ramp up her business. Her biggest challenge was finding clients and scaling her business. She couldn't see how she could train more than one person at a time. I helped her think bigger and tie in not only group trainings but hitting masses of people at one time through corporate trainings and digital products, and by partnering with other health care professionals.

In just four short months working together, Stef achieved amazing results. She doubled the number of her clients, doubled her prices and was on track to triple her business income that year. She went from having one product to adding four more revenue generating income streams, and from no partnerships to having profitable joint ventures with doctors, apartment communities and massage therapists.

Dreams die when we don't plan and prepare, and yet planning and preparation require facing the big question: "How?" How am I going to find the money to do this? How am I going to support my family during this transition? How am I going to find clients? How do I know where to start, and what to do in what order? The "how" is overwhelming when we don't know where to start, so we give up before we get started, or too soon after we make the leap. Sometimes we know what to do, but we don't know when to take each step.

The biggest barrier to leaving a job and following your passions is lack of confidence in your ability to succeed, and the only way to counter that is to get educated about what you need to do. Go talk to people who have already done what you intend to do; meet other people who have succeeded at what you want to do. This will help you to become aware of things you didn't even know to ask about and to identify all of the moving pieces.

When I launch a new venture, I begin by simplifying and organizing. Because I'm very visual, I write everything down and then piece it together. I look at all of my milestones and decide which has to be first, second, third and so on. I make note of which piece I need before I can start this other piece. I break it all down until I know the exact sequence of events, starting with which piece I can take action on *today*.

I said hope is not a strategy. Neither is fear. I let fear drive me for years before I finally realized I would be happier moving *toward* something rather than away from something. Your fear of failure, or fear that you won't know how to do something, or fear that you won't have enough money to quit your job, or fear that others won't approve of your decision to leave the work world—that fear is driving you just as my fear of losing everything drove me. Except in your case, it's *keeping* you from following your calling.

If you want to escape your job, give yourself an advantage. Put yourself in the best position so you can follow your heart and see it through. Life is too short to be stuck doing things you dislike, or things you like but don't really *love*. Take action now to build the life you desire. It is so possible, but you have to start.

If the thought of leaving a job to follow your dreams keeps bubbling up inside you, listen. When you have the right steps in place, you can leave successfully. Decide to do it. Commit to taking action. Believe you can do it. Act.

Don't just dream the dream; *do the dream*.

Nancy Gaines is the CEO of Gain Advantages, Inc. and an international podcaster on the Women Gaining Wealth *show. She consulted with Fortune 500 companies for decades and launched three of her own companies; her business perspective is extensive in scope, geography and industry. Nancy uses this experience and knowledge to help business owners be highly profitable, achieve their vision and reach financial milestones by mirroring larger corporations' practices.*

As a national keynote speaker, bestselling author and business expert, Nancy guides and mentors above-average achievers to grow their businesses to gain a competitive advantage. Her signature product is the Accelerated VIP Strategy Session that enhances business creativity, inspiration and success. CEOs and entrepreneurs work with her to get clarity, develop plans on next best steps, create a strategic road map to implement solutions to their toughest business challenges and have access to Nancy's network and mentors. Her core talent of simplification shows people how they can save time and money by doing things more strategically and efficiently.

Nancy enjoys being active by hiking, skiing, running and volunteering. Listen to her international podcast, the Women Gaining Wealth *show on iTunes; follow @NancyLGaines on Twitter; visit the website at www.NancyGaines.com.*

B. Heather Pinard

THE POWER OF WORDS

Have you ever found yourself saying mean things but can't seem to stop yourself? Have you ever cried over what you later thought was nothing important? Have you laughed for no apparent reason, or during inappropriate times? Have you ever been inpatient or quick tempered and wondered why you couldn't control it? Have you ever felt sad when you received good news?

If you answered "yes" to any of these questions, you are not alone. The reason you sometimes feel or behave in ways that seem incongruent to what is happening in your life is because very often your thoughts and feelings are not your own. The thoughts *seem* like your thoughts and the feelings *feel* like your feelings, but in truth many of your thoughts and feelings were imposed on you before you were old enough to be aware it was happening.

From a young age we are bombarded with images, thoughts and words that are not our own, and yet we believe they are true because they come from our peers, the television, someone we trust. Those who impart this information are unaware of what they are doing because they themselves had the same thing happen to them, as did their parents, and their grandparents and so on. Some say this process of imparting information begins in the womb.

In his book *VALIS*, Philip K. Dick said, "There exists, for everyone, a sentence—a series of words—that has the power to destroy you. Another sentence exists, another series of words, that could heal you. If you're lucky you will get the second, but you can be certain of getting the first."

I received variations on the first sentence—the one that could destroy me—on a regular basis for more than six years. The bullying began when I attended a French school run by nuns. I was the only American student, and the nuns did not have a favorable opinion of Americans. The students followed their example, and soon the nuns and the students were both engaged in tormenting

The bullying began when I attended a French school run by nuns.

me. The nuns took every chance to punish me for even minor infringements of the rules; the switch, the ruler and the dunce cap were their instruments of torture.

The next year I got very ill. I now know it was because my body was under so much stress that my immunity was down. I was open to dis-ease. For nine months I had to be on bedrest twenty-four hours a day, seven days a week. My parents hired a tutor to help me keep up with my studies. Even though I was very ill and hurt in every joint so that I had to teach myself to relax one joint at a time or else the pain was too excruciating to go to sleep at night; even though I almost died from a high fever that would not go down; even though it hurt badly when my mother exercised my legs so that I would not develop atrophy, I loved the fact I did not have to go to school. *Anything to keep me out of school is worth it,* I thought.

When we moved I was excited. I thought things were going to be different in the new school. To my surprise, things were even worse, as these were Americans tormenting, bullying and picking on an American. But they didn't know I had been bullied for years and had reached my limit.

At age eleven, I took my life back. I can remember the incident as if it were yesterday. It was one of those rare beautiful spring days when the air is crisp and it's not too hot yet. We were all in in shirts and had been able to go to school without our bulky jackets. It had been a hard winter, and the warmth of the sun felt lovely through my clothing.

That day, I was surrounded by a group of my peers who did not want me there, but also would not let me leave. They made fun of my strong French accent and laughed at me. I was getting more and more agitated and upset by the second. I wanted to respond, however, the more agitated I became, the more I had problems remembering American words. Under the pressure of their taunts, French words tumbled out of my mouth, which only led to more teasing.

The ringleader of the group of bullies was the principal's daughter. She made it clear that, if I told the principal how she and the others were treating me, her mother wouldn't believe me and would not take any action. I remember thinking, *Will I have*

**I took that blame inside of me and let it
hold me back from living life full out.**

---

to endure this forever? Would I be made fun of all the time? Is it worth living, if all I have to look forward to is this constant barrage of abuse, of being made the butt of all the jokes? I felt sick. Mother always reminded me of the old rhyme, "sticks and stones may break your bones, but names will never hurt you." But I knew all too well that rhyme was wrong. Their words *did* hurt.

I had had enough! As one of the boys approached me intent on taunting me further, I didn't wait to hear what he had to say. I gathered all of my strength and socked him in the nose. His eyes wide; he fell to the ground. His nose was bleeding. Someone ran to the principal's office, and when she came to see what had happened, she asked me follow her to her office.

I knew I was about to be expelled. Fortunately, my one and only friend spoke up for me. At first the principal didn't believe her, and at that point I thought the principal's daughter was right, I might as well give up. However, after questioning other witnesses, she accepted my story as truth. I felt vindicated. Finally someone could help me make it all go away. I was relieved. From then on her daughter and I had an uneasy truce, until I moved to the International School where I felt safe and at home.

At age eleven I was able to recognize that the words my bullies used against me were hurtful and also do something about it. I had made a decision not to be a victim anymore and take my life back. Now imagine if all of this had happened when I was a baby or a small child, when I could not discern truth from fiction, and I certainly could not defend myself. Do you see how words and images are imprinted on our psyche from an early age?

It's not just the words we hear that have an impact on us; it is also the words we don't hear. Even before I endured years of bullying, I was molested. Today, we would call it rape. My parents never talked about the incident. As a result, I grew up believing it

Avoid using the word 'try.' It is a secret self-sabotaging word that will set you up to fail.

was my fault. I took that blame inside of me and let it hold me back from living life full out, and from believing I was worthy of success, happiness, any good thing. Later I became an over-achiever. I graduated college magna cum laude and with my Master's degree in education summa cum laude, intent on doing it all. And yet somehow, there was always a nagging feeling that prevented me from going all in.

About twenty-one years ago, my body started to fall apart again. I had one foot on a banana peel and one foot in the grave. I wanted to crawl into bed and never get out. I hurt all over, so much that I had to give up my teaching position. Instead of staying in bed, I went to visit our daughter and grandson. On the way, I met some friends who had a product that helped me turn my life around. They also had a course, Humans Being More, that was my first insight into the mind-body connection.

While taking this and other classes, I discovered the part the rape played in my subconscious and how it was holding me back. I asked my mother, "Why didn't you ever talk to me about it?"

My mother said, "You were so young. We thought you had forgotten about it and we didn't want to dredge up old wounds."

Wow! Nearly my entire life I thought I was to blame for being raped, and I hadn't broached the subject with my parents either. At first I felt hurt, but then I realized my parents were raised in a different time when talking about such subjects was taboo. I knew they did what they thought was best for me with the knowledge they had at the time.

Over the next few years I took various courses covering many disciplines, became certified to teach and conducted my own research that took me to new levels of understanding about the mind-body connection. I became a keen observer of people and the words they used. I identified words that caused people to stay in their comfort zone—the same words I was using to stay in mine. I found answers to many questions and I was able to resolve them.

For the past ten years my mission has been helping people overcome their thoughts, emotions, feelings and suppressed experiences. We begin by first gaining awareness of the issue, and then we neutralize subconscious and conscious beliefs so we can make conscious decisions to take action and achieve the lifestyles of our highest visions.

Whether you remember the experiences, words and images from your childhood or not, everything that happened to you as a child is in your subconscious. Your subconscious knows and it is protecting you from anything that may be painful. Yet that protection contributes to holding you back from living the full life you were meant to live.

Think about where you are. Are you stuck? Are you under stress? The real cause of these thoughts, feelings and words has nothing to do with you. It is not your fault. Stop blaming yourself.

However, now that you know, it is your responsibility to gain awareness of the past and stop its negative impact on your present and your bright future. It is up to you to take control. Think of the opportunities lost if you do nothing. Think of the anguish you still have.

Get out of your own way. Learn a new way of thinking. Get rid of the images, thoughts and words imposed on you by others without your consent.

Beginning this process may seem overwhelming, so I'm going to give you one tip that will help you immensely, no matter if you ever take a class or consult with me or another coach about these issues. Avoid using the word "try." It is a secret self-sabotaging word that will set you up to fail. The definition of the word "try" is to "make an attempt or effort to do something." Where in that definition do you see a call to action? Instead, the word calls on you to *attempt* something. Not to do, but to *try*. Right from the start your mind and body knows that you may not achieve it.

The word is letting you off the hook even before you begin. Recognize your use of this word and replace it whenever possible. Then, watch how your life changes when that word is removed from your thought and speech patterns.

Alan W. Watts said, "We seldom realize, for example that our most private thoughts and emotions are not actually our own. For we think in terms of languages and images which we did not invent, but which were given to us by our society." When you begin to strip away the words, images and thoughts that control your life you will be introduced to a new world where getting out of your own way is as easy as taking a step to the left or right. It is time to start (or re-start) your journey of self-discovery!

B. Heather Pinard was born overseas and lived most of her life outside the United States. She holds a Master's degree in education and studied with such masters as T. Harv Eker, Adam Markel, Brian Tracy, Larry Proffit, Heidi and Joel Roberts, Bob Proctor, Blair Singer and Zig Zigler. She is certified in applied kinesiology, the study of body movement and the emotion code. Connect with Heather at www.StopAndLetGo.com.

Claudia Bethlem

THE PLACE YOU ALWAYS WANTED TO BE

If I could, I would stay under water forever. The ocean welcomes me back as I explore the world below the surface, magical in its vast wonders. My mind is quiet; almost at once I am totally at peace. *I am in the place I always wanted to be.*

I'm reminded of the apnea diving I used to do, which required me to lower my heartbeat to a minimum, focus on my breath and use the least amount of energy necessary to stay as long as possible underwater. It was the reason I became interested in meditation. For me, diving is Nirvana.

Even this moment, snorkeling with sailing charter guests off the Brazilian coast is a meditation of sorts. I could get lost in my own moment, but this journey has to be guided. I keep an eye on them, but give our guests the freedom to explore and do what they want. I know they're reunited with their childlike wonder here, far from the stresses of every day life. I know they are healing. I know they are reconnecting to self, to soul and to heart. I know, because I am here because I too reconnected to my self, my soul and my heart.

By the age of forty-two, I had money, power and a prominent job as a Health, Safety and Environment Specialist (HSE) for the gas and oil industry. Yet, when I looked at myself in the mirror, I could hardly recognize myself. My passion is exploring and preserving nature's wonders, but my daily work life was nothing like what I envisioned when I set forth on my path to become a marine biologist. I worked with people with whom I had nothing in common. I was bitter. I felt older than my years, and my health was awful.

I decided to change everything. I left my job and went to Patagonia, Chile for two months to exercise and to think. Then one night, when I was camping, I had a dream. In the dream I built

---

I felt older than my years, and
my health was awful.

---

something very odd. I was working with people, showing them the sea, and they all seemed to like it very much. More than that, I was somehow helping them come back to happiness and to connect with nature.

In the dream, I also saw an underwater observatory. When I woke up, the details of the dream were still vivid in my mind. Once I could reach an Internet connection, I searched for similar structures online. I was surprised to discover the observatory really existed! I thought, "If the structure I saw in my dream exists, then why not the rest of my dream?"

During my time in Chile, I met a lama from Tibet and a mentor. They taught me how to feed my "white wolf" instead of my "black wolf." You might recognize this analogy from Native American healing stories. The white wolf represents positive emotions, such as joy, love and contentment, while the black wolf represents negative emotions such as guilt, sadness and anger.

The white wolf is the part of us that is compassionate, generous and empathetic; the black wolf is jealous, arrogant and resentful. While the white wolf practices self-love, faith and gratitude, the black wolf practices self-pity and greed. Where the white wolf is optimistic in thoughts and deeds, the black wolf thinks only of negative outcomes and fears, and acts accordingly. The two wolves live inside all of us, my mentors explained. The wolf we feed, wins.

They also taught me that my life was a projection of my inner self. I learned that I could change my entire life simply by changing the way I saw things. I started slowly building a plan that would gradually bring me the expertise to move on the project of my dream: showing people how to deeply love the ocean, and bringing awareness to the environment and to their own dreams.

I would visualize it every day and then I wrote a plan for the project and started executing it. Most of my dreams become reality when I put them on paper and start assigning dates, responsibilities and timelines. I trained to become a coach so I could help the guests we would serve on our sailing excursions. I knew I could succeed, because I received powerful and effective teams and a set of daily practices to empower myself. Slowly, I prepared myself to bring my dream into reality.

On our first expedition, we drove from Rio de Janeiro on the beautiful green coast road up to Angra dos Reis, and set sail for Ilha Grande (Big Island). As the sailboat pulled away from the shore, I felt peace wash over me. As I said at the start of this chapter, I am

I could change my entire life simply by changing the way I saw things.

crazy about being in the water. When I looked forward at the vast expanse of ocean, and looked back to my crew and our chartered guests, I realized for the first time: *This is the place I always wanted to be.*

I feel this every time I take a new group out on for an expedition. I wonder how many people can say that about their work, to know without a doubt that they have found their place on this planet, the place where they are both making a difference in the world and living according to their own true happiness.

Snorkeling, sunset picnics, star gazing; sport activities, yoga, meditation; healthy gastronomic delights, inner work, coaching, biodiversity—it is all as I envisioned in my dream, except made better by passionate and careful planning, and the input from mentors and my crew. I am mindful that I am living the life of my *actual dreams*, playing out the beautiful picture I envisioned three years ago, sleeping on the ground in a tent in Chile.

When we trek through the rainforest to a beautiful waterfall, we walk the trail in silence, listening to the sounds of the howling monkeys, the parrots and the maritacas. We connect to the sounds and nothing else. At a little lake, we meditate at the rocks

The sea works magic on people's hearts.

and release every unwanted thought that might be left behind. I guide our guests toward being conscious of the people they are, their strengths and dreams and then walk back to the waterfall to cleanse and let go.

Back at the boat, we have to convince people to leave, because it's time to sail back to the marina. I never want to go back to Rio. I could stay out on the water forever, but even when I am in Rio, I keep the feeling in my heart. I feel the sun inside of me, the different states of water—sometimes turbulent, sometimes peaceful. The water is like our emotions; Get in touch with them, recognize what you want, and you will be connected to your inner motivation.

The sea works magic on people's hearts; it helps to melt them, so the work can be done more deeply. The career I had before I started taking people on holistic expeditions was vital for the environment, yes. But I was feeding an industry that could not nurture me in return. I was feeding a false idea of myself, the black wolf inside of me. Many of our charter guests have similar stories. The details may be different, but inside their wolves are battling away. By the time they have finished their short journey with us, they have begun to learn how to feed the white wolf within, and the white wolf is winning.

I go underwater, and I am aware of the expanse of the world beneath the surface. In this, nature's lesson, I see that we are bigger, more powerful, stronger and wise than we think we are—than we are *supposed* to think we are. Beneath the surface, there is a vast ocean of promise within you. Will you dive beneath? Will you make your vivid dream a reality, so we all may benefit? Breathe. Take it all in. You are about to find the place you always wanted to be.

Claudia Bethlem is the founder of Immerse, a sailing charter offering expeditions focused on body, mind and spirit off the coast of Brazil. Skippers with more than eighty thousand miles of experience in the Caribbean, Tahiti, Europe and the Brazilian Coast captain well-equipped boats; great chefs, pampering crews and marine biologists provide exclusive excursions to learn about local biodiversity and to connect with the sunny side of life. Immerse works with corporations, families, fitness instructors and coaches to provide custom experiences for guests.

As a Health, Safety and Environment Specialist (HSE), Claudia has developed and implemented an extensive portfolio of activities, including audit, senior strategic consulting, training and coaching; she has extensive expertise in HSE management systems for the oil and gas industry. She holds an MSc degree in oceanography, graduated with a major in biology from Santa Ursula University in Rio de Janeiro in 1990, and received her MS at FURG, Fundacao Universidade do rio Grande in 1998.

Claudia has worked in the conservation of endangered species field for fifteen years, collaborating on projects to preserve the following biodiversity "hot spots:" Abrolhos National Marine Park, Fernando de Noronha National Marine Park, Tamar Project, South Shetland Islands, Weddel Ocean and Gerlache Strait in Antarctica. Claudia ventured into the travel industry and started Immerse in 2012. The Brazilian coast is beautiful and Claudia wants others to experience it, to come and touch it, feel it, breathe it, and most importantly—learn from it—so that we can all keep it beautiful and pristine for years to come. To connect with Claudia, visit www.ImmersExpeditions.com/en.

Marty Matika

PERSPECTIVE IS EVERYTHING

*"Only one thing has to change for us to know happiness
in our lives: where we focus our attention."*
Greg Anderson

Lying in my twin bed, with the house quiet and my mother asleep in the next room, I stared at the ceiling and plotted. *Maybe if I promise to be the best kid in the world*, I thought. *How could they refuse that? Who wouldn't want their good kid to be an even* better *kid? How is that not an attractive proposal? I'll be a perfect angel.*

I was five years old when my parents divorced and I began my campaign to get them back together. For years I was relentless in my efforts to make my family whole again and heal my broken heart. I was manipulative and charming. I played on their sympathies.

I'd say to my mom, "Is there any possibility we can work this out? I'll do whatever it takes to get you back together." Or to my dad, "I don't want to lose the family, Can you please work it out with Mom?"

Maybe because she was afraid of hurting my feelings, Mom shut me down but left a kernel of hope by saying, "Maybe someday." Dad, on the other hand, simply said, "It's just not going to happen. I'm sorry."

The dynamics in my family were so different after my parents split up, and I just wanted a happy, complete family—my mother and father under one roof. I was so envious of my friends whose parents stayed together. I'd look at them and think, *Man, I wish my parents would have stayed together. I miss being able to do things with Dad when I want and with Mom when I want.*

I finally gave up on reuniting my family when my dad told me he planned to remarry. I was thirteen years old and I believed I had failed. The divorce had wreaked havoc in my life, and I thought

I was relentless in my efforts to make my family whole again.

I had nobody to help me through the pain. All of those years of holding out hope and trying to get my parents back together were in vain. The heartbreak I felt when they split up—the loss of trust, the loss of love—came barreling back into my life and sent me down a dangerous road.

I started to tell myself, "You're not good enough to make a difference in Mom's and Dad's lives, so you can't make a difference in other people's lives."

For years I had felt disconnected from God, because "He" didn't prevent the divorce from happening. After my dad remarried, I wrote off God completely—and everyone else. *There's no one to help me. This is a living hell.*

It was only when I started working with a therapist who understood my world that things started to get better. I finally had someone in my corner who got me, someone who could help me process my feelings of intense pain and anger. Fortunately, I started therapy when I was still a teenager and was able to find some relief before I did major damage to my life and my future.

Therapy was a game changer. To be seen, to be heard, to be understood—it was empowering. From that healing place, I was able to deal with the trauma of my parent's divorce and begin to focus on my *own* well-being, not their "reunion." Being a child of divorce would not define me.

I started exploring self-development work, like Landmark Education, and reading books and attending different types of workshops. Norman Vincent Peale's *The Power of Positive Thinking,* among others, helped me turn around my negative thinking. I finally realized, *I can succeed. I can start to love and trust others again.* I learned to be positive about my circumstances, to make the best of what I had in my life and accept what I didn't have without letting it hold me back. It was a process that was painful at times, but the reward was the ability to re-create my life.

As a counselor and youth empowerment specialist, my mission is to help young people whose parents are divorced break free from suffering and trauma and create the life they want. According to the article, "When Parents Break Sacred Vows: the Role of Spiritual Appraisals, Coping, and Struggles in Young Adults' Adjustment to

Perspective is everything.

Parental Divorce (Warner, Heidi L.; Mahoney, Annette; Krumrei, Elizabeth J. *Psychology of Religion and Spirituality,* Vol 1(4), Nov 2009, 233-248), studies show that "adolescents that experienced spiritual struggles over the divorce reported higher current depression, and anxiety" and saw "life through the filter of divorce."

Research argues that for adolescents whose parents have divorced, life can go one of two ways: The circumstances of the divorce can either bring success into their life or can be a detriment to their life. How the adolescent views the situation is critical.

With respect to my own experience, when my family "broke up," I did view it as a sacred loss, though I could not have articulated that at the time. I was devastated, and saw only one way out of my pain: to reunite my parents. When I finally realized that would never happen, I saw only failure and more loss. And that perspective caused me to spiral down into a dark place.

Perspective is everything. In my practice, I challenge my clients to shift their perspectives about whatever situation they are in, because they always have a choice to look at something pessimistically or optimistically. Cognitive therapy teaches us that thinking creates results. When you look at something

> *There is no pain that human beings can't overcome.*

pessimistically and start telling yourself, "I can't do this," you can't. When you're perspective is "I have no power," you don't. And when you tell yourself, "I won't be able to move past this," you won't.

Thinking leads to feelings, which leads to actions, which leads to behaviors. If you're thinking negatively, your feelings will become negative—anger, anxiety, sadness. Experiencing these feelings on a regular basis will lead to acting out, possibly sabotaging relationships and opportunities that come into your life. Over time, this will become a pattern—this will become *your life*. Thinking creates your world and creates your reality. A lot of the time, we can't even see that this faulty thinking is running the show. That's why I believe it is so important to work with a professional to help you see where your thinking may be leading you to undesirable results in your life.

The simple shift to thinking positively about your situation can turn things around. A lot of kids don't notice the undercurrent of negative thoughts and feelings in their lives. They act out, not realizing that they are responding to feelings of anger, or mistrust of others or lack of love for themselves or others.

One of my clients is a teenager dealing with his parents' separation. When I met Dale he was really shut down and closed off. He didn't want to talk. We worked on processing some of the issues and pain he's experienced so that it would not define him, or own him—so it would not ruin his life. I said, "It's okay to feel the feelings, but don't let them eat you up. What are you going to do about it?"

Now that Dale has been able to work through some of these feelings, and has made the decision to define his life on his own terms, he's turned his whole life around. He gets As and Bs in school, excels in sports and has become a responsible kid who is building new, healthy relationships. By processing the trauma of his parents' separation, Dale has been able to make good choices and stay open to discovering what he loves, and what he might want to pursue in life.

You often can't change the circumstances you are dealt, but you can change the way you view these circumstances. You can't do anything about parents separating—children have no say in it. I was five years old and tried everything I could think of to change the outcome, but it was out of my hands. I had to shift my perspective and come to realize, "My parents are who they are—who am I going to be?" This is taking responsibility—not for the situation itself, but for how I react to it, which is the only thing I could control.

This approach is helpful for dealing with other crises, such as tragic accidents that are beyond your control. And it is helpful in dealing with the past, which is over and done with and cannot be altered. Another client, Rachel, came in to see me in a deep depression stemming from trauma she experienced as a child and her kids growing up and getting ready to leave the house. She had felt like a victim her entire life, and believed she couldn't do anything to get the results she wanted. A stay-at-home mom, Rachel's great passion was acting, but she had given it up more than two decades before.

We worked together for several months, clearing the "cobwebs out of her closet." With my help, she processed old hurts and shifted her perspective about how the traumatic experiences of the past shaped her in positive ways, in the skills and compassion she developed as a result. Then, we shifted her perspective of her current "circumstances."

Rachel believed she couldn't pursue her life's purpose because she didn't have time or support. She said, "There's only so much

I can do. I have to spend time with the kids, and take care of the house." Her husband was behind her one hundred percent, but she still couldn't see how it would ever be possible to live her dream.

The first thing we looked at was using affirmations to change her perspective to a more empowering one. If you can retrain your brain to start thinking positively, your perspective will start to become brighter.

In addition, sometimes shifting perspective is a simple matter of looking at options, to see beyond your perceived limitations. Rachel worked on building a framework of support so she could pursue acting. For example, she hired a cleaning person and enlisted other parents to help her pick up and drop off kids from practices.

I said, "Take one action this week. Join a local play. Find an agent. Something."

Within a couple of months, Rachel landed her first paid TV commercial and a lead part in a play! Put to the wayside for twenty years, her dreams are back and in full force! She has never been happier and she is extremely grateful.

There is no pain that human beings can't overcome if they are willing to do the emotional work it takes to get to the other side. The "other side" is so freeing, so rewarding. I felt trapped by my circumstances for years, and when I finally took responsibility for my *perspective* about those circumstances and broke out of my victim mentality, I had the power to change my life for the better. I have eternal thanks for the therapists and coaches who helped me work through this traumatic time, and I pay it forward by helping other young people who are children of divorced parents do the same.

Perspective is everything. We can make up any story we want about our circumstances. Why not make up something empowering that inspires us and makes us feel good?

Marty Matika, MS, is a counselor and youth empowerment specialist. He is the founder of Life Circles, a practice providing counseling, coaching and divorce support for individuals and families. Marty specializes in helping young people who are going through the stressful and traumatic experience of their parents' divorce. He offers one-on-one sessions, as well as workshops, in the Philadelphia area. To connect with Marty and get a free copy of The Top Five Warning Signs to Notice in a Young Person Suffering as a Result of Divorce, *visit www. Life-Circles.com.*

Diane Deal

SOMETHING MORE

The truth will set you free, but first it will piss you off.
Gloria Steinem

Ifelt as though I was entering the gates of an amusement park. My senses were on overload. Even the airplane fuel smelled delightful when mixed with the cacophony of children's squeals and the wheels on the jet way. What a difference six months can make!

For my first foray into the world after a long and solitary illness, I had attended a three-day event in my hometown. I'd had to stay in the hotel where the event was being held, as I was too ill to make the half-hour return trip. I recalled the frenetic pace of my packing as I mentally checked off items on my must-pack list. The heating pad, eight medications, sinus rinses, vitamins and herbs. Now my only accompaniments were a cashmere scarf, a small backpack and my trusty carry-on for a twelve-day trip.

The smell of newly minted plane and the latest technology welcomed me with open arms. This was the maiden voyage of the Dreamliner and my maiden voyage since having a constant chaperone for all travel in the last five years. My skin tingled and a grin was plastered on my face as I walked up the aisle and was warmly greeted by a smartly dressed flight attendant.

"Fasten your seat belts; you are in for an amazing journey," the attendant shouted. It was very fortuitous: London and Dr. Richard Bandler, NLP (neuro-linguistic programming) founder and trainer, calling me on to the next phase of my life. I sat back and relaxed and felt extremely grateful to be alive, replete with the knowledge that things can and do change.

It is the life-defining moments, the ones that almost break you that can have the greatest impact. My physical and mental decline began when I was a newly divorced mom with three growing

I was sucked into a vortex of negativity and victim mentality.

boys, and no formal education or means of support. I lay awake at night, my heart pounding, consumed by anxiety. Out of those restless nights came a determination to find my way to a better life. I enrolled in college and visualized myself in a cap and gown with my kids cheering for me and a home filled with all of the things we always dreamed of. This dream and the support from friends and family fueled me. I had a passion and a purpose. In ten years, I succeeded and went to work at a Fortune 500 company with a starting salary equal to what I would have made in five years at my previous job.

My climb up the ladder was fraught with perils, late nights, working weekends. I'd chosen a profession that provided my family with an excellent income, a new home and a rental property. I travelled to exotic locales. However, I soon began to live in a constant state of stress and to experience more and more frequent sinus infections until the only solution was surgery. *How could my career be skyrocketing but my health declining and my happiness levels at an all time low? Wasn't this the life I always dreamed about? Why wasn't I happy and healthy? Was I suffering from a mental illness? Dying?* I couldn't put my finger on it. Have you ever fallen victim to this type of analysis?

I finally had surgery to correct my persistent and debilitating sinus infections, after suffering with them for five miserable years. I thought, *This is it. The surgery will cure this problem and everything will be better.* Except it wasn't. The infections persisted, confounding my doctors and causing me to enter a deep depression.

When I was laid off from my job, I was sucked into a vortex of negativity and victim mentality. It took every ounce of energy I had to fight off the constant infection that I called "the alien," who repeatedly punched me in the head. Her malicious tentacles stole my energy and my thoughts. I was convinced this was the end. Sirens blaring and lights flashing the ambulance arrived, and at that moment I made a deal with God: "If I survive, I will do something amazing."

I had emergency surgery to repair a previously botched sinus procedure and had a second operation to have a non-cancerous brain tumor removed. These surgeries and the frequency and

I had to find a way to honor my promise.

duration of my previous infections and surgeries led to a mild-to-moderate cognitive decline that continues today.

During this period, my mom was diagnosed with Alzheimer's. Watching her deteriorate and lapse into a hollow shell, void of all emotion, and seeing her inability to recognize her family, I spiraled into a deeper depression. I couldn't move off the couch. TV characters became my friends. Most of my friends and family stopped talking to me or coming to visit. I was no fun to be around. I let my disease define me. The final blow came when I was unable to eulogize my parents due to the fear that I would stare blankly at the congregation, unable to speak.

I had to find a way to honor my promise. To get me out of my funk I was invited to a Peak's Potential seminar. This was my first stay outside of my house in seven years, and even though the hotel was close by, I lugged enough medical supplies in my suitcase to survive for weeks. The metaphor was not lost on me, and I thought, *This is crazy.*

At the seminar, I was fortunate to have Adam Markel as my trainer. He discussed rising above fear and not letting fear rule our lives and he talked about searching inside for answers. I always

---

I experienced the life-changing effects gratitude can have.

---

knew the spiritual aspect of me was there, but I had long decided I would not lead with the heart until I was physically well. Adam's words helped me realize, *Maybe I'm not going to get well* until *I do some of that heart work. Maybe I'm sacrificing what is important for what is urgent.* That was the start, my little nugget of, "huh."

I attended another seminar a couple of months later; my suitcase was still packed with my mini-pharmacy. I knew had to shut my brain off and focus on what my heart wanted, the bigger picture, connecting to spirit, but it still hadn't clicked for me. Being an analytical person, I was unfamiliar with what I considered "woo-woo," but I took a leap of faith and pleaded with the universe to send me a sign. I begged to be passionate about something.

One day I was guided along a hiking path I hadn't taken in years. I came upon what I thought was a branch but when the snake slithered across the path I didn't freak out, as I normally would; I was terrified of snakes. I thought, *This is my opportunity to not let fear rule me.* I watched it for a moment and thought about my mom and her fear of snakes and our shared experience with cognitive decline. I sat down a nearby rock and started to cry. When I returned home, I searched my book on animal spirits and their meaning. I wasn't surprised to learn snakes symbolized transformation, but the passage still gave me goose bumps.

I realized, *I can't go back to climbing the corporate ladder. I need something. Something* else. *Something* more. Suddenly, I was asking, *How do I serve?* I had never had that thought before. I began to feel a stirring of passion. An article about Pete Frates, a former college baseball star and the inspiration for the ALS Ice Bucket Challenge, further moved me to find a way to honor my mom by helping others also suffering from cognitive decline. It's seems crazy that in one day I overcame a major fear and stumbled upon my purpose. Inspiration can come in many forms and from the unlikeliest of places. That snake truly *was* a sign of transformation.

I had witnessed my mom's decline from a life rich with love for life and passion for all things family, to sitting in a chair alone. Wasn't I in the same situation? Hadn't my isolation compounded my issues? I began my training with Peak Potentials where I connected with others in similar situations. I sought connection through commonality and compassion.

I experienced the life-changing effects gratitude can have. I am now grateful for my illness as it led me to my passion. I'm no longer embarrassed by my story, but I see it as a way to inspire others. I am here not to take but to serve. My wish for you is that you will never stop searching for your passion and when you find it, as I know you will, you will feel the wonder, joy and love for who you are, what you are about to create—and hang on, it will be a wild ride!

There are days when the blackout shades on my mind close early and I can feel the sand washing away under my feet. My mind is like a chalkboard with phrases and words continually in motion. I am passionate about sharing my experiences, hundreds of hours of research, new and exciting advancements in "brain health," and about my work with top neurologists. I am learning and changing my brain and my outlook. My health and happiness continue to improve.

There is much stigma and a lack of understanding surrounding dementia. There is no script or process for how to heal your brain. It is my intention to correct this by being part of the solution.

It still amazes me that I was able to transform my life so quickly. After seven years living in agony, my entire life and future compromised, in the span of seven *months* I became a completely different person. In February I was lying around, unable and unwilling to leave the house. By October, I was on that flight to London by myself, my bags not stuffed with pills and curative agents, but packed with favorite things and possibilities. This is the power of heart-centered transformation.

Diane Deal has a BS in technical communication and psychology and a project management certificate from CSU. She has more than twenty years' experience as a technical writer and software project/program manager for a Fortune 500 company. She is a bestselling author and a Licensed Master Practitioner of NLP and a graduate of Jon Kabat Zinn's Mindfulness Based Stress Reduction program. She is currently living her passion.

Her mother's diagnosis with early onset Alzheimer's disease and her own cognitive impairment led Diane to develop a program for those suffering from genetic-, age- or lifestyle-induced cognitive impairment. This program and companion book, Stop the Decline, *are due out in 2016. The book focuses on seven key areas: cognitive training, physical activity, socialization, nutrition, detoxification, lifestyle and prevention. Topics include: NLP strategies; environmental and relationship toxicity; brain nourishment, plasticity and immunology and stress reduction and mindfulness.*

Diane's mission statement is: "To contribute to the world by designing cutting-edge programs that pair science, common sense, motivational empowerment and NLP techniques to nourish the mind and advance humankind." Connect with Diane at DianeDeal.com.

Sabra Sasson

DREAM A DIFFERENT DREAM

We were at war.

When I finally garnered the strength to file for divorce against my husband, I was sad but relieved. I wanted to be married to someone who appreciated me for me, who wanted to build a life together, and I didn't have that with my husband. I knew I had to end the pain and gather myself so I had a chance of experiencing real love and having a family.

Having suffered through countless attempts to resolve difficult issues almost from the beginning of our brief marriage, I had agonized over the decision. I thought following through with filing for divorce would be the hardest part. Unfortunately, it was only the beginning.

Married only nineteen months, we held no property together, nor did we have children. Under normal circumstances, our divorce should have been easy to settle. It should have been simple. Unfortunately, my soon-to-be ex-husband was bitter and intentionally made every step of the process difficult. But he wasn't the only person holding up the process. I wanted it all: I wanted to move on with my life, but I also wanted to "right" all of the "wrongs" that happened in my marriage.

What followed was months of litigation, frustration and heartache; many court appearances, and too many motions filed to count. I was consumed with the divorce; my job as a real estate attorney was my only reprieve from the stress and negativity.

My attorneys frequently reminded me, "Focus on the end result, Sabra—the divorce judgment, not your idea of justice."

Still, despite my desire to be free, I couldn't let go of my need to be right. I held on to my conviction despite all of it: hearing our "dirty laundry" aired in court; watching the man I once

---

I was consumed with the divorce.

---

loved turn into a contemptuous and vindictive person; enduring a seemingly endless process of discovery, numerous motions and court appearances. He was unreasonable and didn't want to let me go.

One day, while in a negotiation room in court, my ex said, "I will gladly drag this out and take away all of your baby-making years."

At that point I knew I needed to take back my life and my time and finish the divorce once and for all. I stopped focusing on being right and let my attorneys do their job so I could move on to the next chapter in my life. I was happy to trade "having it all" for starting over, no matter what I had to give up to get there.

Eventually, after surviving humiliation of all kinds, stress and anxiety, I came out of my marriage with my head held high. When the dust settled, I realized, if my "simple" divorce was so painful, it must be even more painful for my clients who have assets or children or both.

I thought, *This is what I want to do with my law practice.*

Suddenly I knew what I was meant to do with my life: to help and serve others who are on the difficult path of divorce; to hold their hand through the process so they are supported with care and understanding; and to empower them to make different choices. To help couples dream a different dream.

That was more than ten years ago, and since then I have helped hundreds of couples avoid unnecessary pain, stress and sleepless nights and end their marriage harmoniously. My specialty is mediation. I guide couples so that they let go of their positions going in to the process—positions often rooted in a need for justice, or to win, or in a past hurt—and take a step back to consider what they really want and what they really need in order to build a new future.

In my experience, both personally and professionally, when you operate from a place of needing to be right, you're really not operating from a place of truth. You're focused on where you are today, not where you want to be. Months or years from now, you may look back on a decision you made from that "battle" place and realize you were acting to spite someone, or to feel vindicated, but that your decision didn't serve your best interests.

Acting on a knee-jerk response, especially in the case of a divorce or separation that is highly emotional, may not get you the outcome you want. It may not get you closer to your new

---

I couldn't let go of my need to be right.

---

dream. When you enter into a divorce, the need to be right hinders negotiation. It is through negotiation that you have a chance to achieve an outcome that is the most harmonious for you, your ex and your family.

Wanting to serve more people than I could in my practice, I am writing a book about the process I use with couples. In *The Harmonious Divorce,* I will detail the mediation process and give my best advice for navigating this important transition. A lot of people believe that the only way to get a divorce is to duke it out in the courts, to find a great lawyer who is good at knocking someone out in a fight and race to the courthouse. You don't have to do that. You didn't get married that way, and you don't have to get divorced that way.

You need permission from the state to get married, and you need permission from the state to get divorced, but you don't have to leave a trail of dead bodies to get there.

In mediation training we all study the story about the orange. I'll paraphrase it for you: Two siblings are fighting over one orange. To resolve the dispute, their mother cuts the orange in half and gives each of the children one half. This solution sounds logical and reasonable, except the children were still upset. Had the

When you operate from a place of needing to be right, you're really not operating from a place of truth.

mother made further inquiry she would have discovered that one child wanted the orange for the zest so he can use it to make a pie and the other child was hungry and wanted to enjoy the fruit. Upon learning that, the solution would have become evident— different from the mother's logical belief in the "right" outcome, yet a solution that actually meets the needs and desires of each sibling.

It's similar within divorce cases. Everyone has a position going in, but when we dig a little deeper, we can come up with a solution that truly is a win-win. That "win" may not look like the outcome they envisioned when they walked into the room, but if it is conceived together in mediation, successfully achieving it—and maintaining harmony—is much more likely.

Through mediation I am re-teaching people how to communicate with one another, how to listen and experience being heard. Many of my clients have not been heard by their spouses in a very long time, and many may not even be able to articulate what a positive outcome would be.

When I first meet with clients, they usually want to jump right in and start talking about the issues. One of the first steps in my process is asking them to set all of that aside and spend a few minutes imagining themselves one year after their divorce is finalized. "Where are you living? What are you doing? Where are your kids?" Next, I ask them to share their vision with each other.

Then, we work backwards. I ask, "How are we going to go from where we are right now to where you want to go?"

I do this in my own life. I place my hands over my belly, close my eyes and envision myself going from where I am right now toward my goal or dream, watching myself take all of the necessary steps. I notice how I feel in that moment. If it feels right and I am excited, then I know I'm heading in the right direction.

When we start from the outcome—the different dream—the whole discussion is much easier. Not easy, but *easier*. It's like a road trip. When you set out in your car, you typically don't just start driving. You have your destination in mind, you have your map or GPS, you have a plan about how many stops you'll make along the way. When I mediate clients going through transitions like divorce, we start from the destination (the goal) and create a clear path (from today) toward it.

When ending a relationship or a business, it's important to remember that being right won't necessarily get you where you want to go. In fact, it may steer you in the wrong direction. At the very least, it will delay the process and possibly cause it to be agonizing for all concerned. You have a choice. You can let go of the past, and get the professional help you need to negotiate a new future—on your terms.

No matter what happened in the past, you can achieve a new dream, a different dream. It begins with letting go.

Sabra Sasson, Esq., is an attorney and mediator practicing in New York City. She is the founder and principal of Sabra Law Group, PLLC, a mediation and law practice in midtown Manhattan that offers legal and mediation services to its clients. Sabra handles the legal aspects of major transitions—buying or selling property, planning for marriage or getting divorced—and protects her clients' interests so they can focus on their evolution into this new life change. She employs her skills and experience to help her clients focus on life post-divorce and guides them through the process to get there. For couples embarking on marriage, she helps them protect accumulated assets and create a plan for building assets, wealth and valuables in the future.

Sabra graduated from Brandeis University in 1995 with a Bachelor's in mathematics and minor in education, after which she enrolled in law school and graduated from Hofstra University School of Law in 1998 with her Juris Doctorate. She sat for the bar exam in three states and was thereafter admitted to practice law in New York, New Jersey and Connecticut, and has been practicing law ever since.

Sabra is currently writing a book to guide and empower couples through the process of "uncoupling," The Harmonious Divorce: The Four Step Process to Uncoupling. *Connect with her at www. SabraLawGroup.com.*

David Hibbs

Hope in Unexpected Places

The phrase, "There is always hope" is so common, sometimes I wonder if people even hear it anymore, much less believe it's true. When we encounter unexpected challenges, it's difficult to trust that hope does exist, especially when we are fixated on a specific outcome.

"There's always hope" is not just a pat phrase found on greeting cards or offered up by well-meaning friends. It's a fact. There *is* always hope—but you may not find it by looking straight ahead. You may find it in unexpected ways and places.

My purpose in life is helping entrepreneurs and CEOs rescue their businesses and get everything back on track—sales, systems and finances—so they can turn everything around and come out the other side stronger than ever. Twenty years ago when I started saving lucrative contracts for my corporate employers— earning my employers more than seventy million dollars—I didn't know this was my mission. I only knew I had a knack for project management. It took a layoff and a series of frustrating disappointments and roadblocks to help me see the value of my unique experience and skill set and how to offer it the world.

A few years ago, after thirty years of service, IBM laid me off. At the time, I was so angry. *They're tossing me aside,* I thought, although I knew that they had laid off forty percent of their project managers, worldwide. Yes, I knew it was about the numbers, but because I had started as a customer service tech and worked my way up to management, and because I had earned them millions of dollars and had a one hundred percent success rate as a project manager, I assumed I wouldn't be let go.

After the layoff, I tried to find another project management position, but after several months of unemployment, I still couldn't find a job. I began to feel like a loser, as if all of my problems were caused by me. I started to think, *I'm not good enough. I don't have*

After thirty years of service, IBM laid me off.

---

the right skill set, or enough education, or the right personality people want. The truth was, I had the right skills, and a Master's degree, and had decades of positive feedback from customers—but my mind had started to ignore the facts and play tricks on me. As a result, I became very depressed.

A year later, I made the decision to find something different to do. My sister was a registered nurse, and as I listened to her stories about helping her patients, I realized, *This feeling of helping people is what drew me to project management in the first place.* At the time, I was unable to fulfill someone's need in my field, so I decided to find some other vocation in which I could help someone.

I settled on becoming an Emergency Medical Technician (EMT). First, I volunteered with the local ambulance corps in my town. Then, I applied for a four-month class. I studied hard and busted my behind on the physical fitness portion of the training. I was definitely the oldest in my forty-five-person class! Finally I graduated—at the top of my class. The night I graduated, I applied to the city's contracted medical services company, Rural Metro Medical Services. I was hired three weeks later.

The first few weeks at my new job were tough. I was the "probby," and because I was sixty years old, they officially kept me on probation for six weeks. Still, I was flying high. I had successful transitioned from one career to another. I had found a job that I was good at. My patients appreciated my bedside manner and my coworkers knew they could count on me.

Ten months later, I broke my foot helping a patient onto a gurney in the snow. I went back to work on light duty, and because I was doing a good job in the position, I stayed for eleven months.

When I was finally about to restart the job for which I was initially hired, my doctor found other internal health issues. "You're critically ill, David," he said. "But I'm not sure why."

I was heartbroken.

The day I was supposed to restart my job in the field, I ended up in the hospital as a patient. After a week and eighty-six tests I was told, "You have non-alcoholic cirrhosis of the liver." I was devastated. In an instant, my life changed. Suddenly, the number

---

I had nearly lost the will to continue living.

---

of people focused on my health went from one or two to more than fifteen. With each discussion, whether it was with a doctor, my pastor or my financial advisor, I was warned about decisions or behavior that could prove fatal.

I was laid off and sank further and further into depression and apathy. In a conversation with my financial advisor, I suggested we reduce the size of my term life insurance in order to save money. "Absolutely not," he said. "We need that policy in place when you pass away." I couldn't find the words to respond.

It wasn't until we were driving home that I fell apart. I was sobbing to the point where I had to pull over the car. I told my wife, "I'm sick of people telling me I'm about to die, or that this or that action could prove fatal." In that moment I realized I had nearly lost the will to continue living.

My bad luck continued for a few months—a broken fibula after a fall carrying Christmas decorations to the shed, more depression issues, the inability to do any work around the house due to dizziness caused by my condition. Then one day, my wife encouraged me to attend a Peak Potentials class in Palm Desert,

California. Expecting to be bored, I took a book along and half-listened during the morning session. Then, about mid-afternoon, something caught my attention and I started listening closely to the trainers. The more I listened, the more interested I became.

Over the next few months, I continued to attend personal and professional development trainings. My depression began to lift, and I started taking action on opportunities and ideas. It was a gradual process of coming back to myself, spurred on by a principle I learned at one of my Peaks trainings: "I have important knowledge and experience to share. I add value to people's lives."

All those years I worked as a project manager for IBM, saving contracts and earning them seventy million dollars over and above what was expected—those years were not lost. I had rescued projects for a Fortune 500 company, and I had rescued *myself.* Not

---

No matter what happens, you
always have value.

---

once, but twice. I knew how to get a project back on track, and how to get a life back on track. The work I loved to do didn't have to end just because I was laid off. My value did not end just because I had health issues. In a Peaks training I learned: "I have value, I have always had value, and I can add more value by my actions."

Once I realized that I could continue to do the work I loved, I opened up my own consulting and coaching business. I knew the statistics about startup success and failure rates had only gotten worse over the years and I knew I could help. I set out to help people using my knowledge, my expertise and my additional training as a coach through Peaks.

My first client came to me citing issues with cash flow and lack of a team, but he had bigger problems: He hadn't had a customer in two years. Within six months of working with me, he landed more than seventy clients. Today he is making good money and has completely turned his business around. It was gratifying to watch him transform his company with my guidance and to know

that I had truly found a place for my skills, expertise, knowledge…
and my heart.

Since I opened my company, everything has changed. I still
have health issues, but doctors and tests no longer rule my life.
I feel alive and on purpose, because I am doing what my heart
wants to do. It may take more energy to reach my goals, but I get
there, every time. If I have to climb a mountain, scale a cliff or go
bankrupt to reach a goal, I will do it. I feel passion I haven't felt in
forty years.

It may seem as if I could have transitioned straight into
consulting and opened my own business immediately after I was
downsized. It seems logical, right? But it's not that simple. When
life forces you to step off the trail you know so well, it can be difficult
to give up your plans for the future and chart a new course.

The path to following your heart and truly recognizing your
own value is often long and can have many twists, turns and
roadblocks. If you've been hit with a job loss, illness or one of life's
devastating and unpredictable challenges, keep in mind that, no
matter what happens, you always have value. No one can take
away the person you've become. You may not be able to use your
knowledge and expertise in the same way you used it before your
life changed, but you can find a new way to offer your wisdom and
talents to the world if you remain vulnerable and open to receiving
ideas from unexpected places.

Dust yourself off and look at yourself in the mirror. To that face
looking back at you say, "I have value, I have always had value and
I can add more value by my actions." Say that at least ten times in
the morning, ten times in the afternoon and ten times at night.
Do this every day until you start to see ways to add value to *other*
people's lives. You will know that you are on the right path and
following your heart when the changes you've made uplift your
view of the world, of yourself and of the direction your life has
taken.

Keep yourself in the game. With help you can get to the other
side of whatever challenge or transition you're working through

right now. Be prepared for a new journey, a new direction that may lead to a new you!

Dave Hibbs is the CEO and director of new business opportunities of Hibbs Services, LLC, a company offering business consulting/ analysis and coaching. Through his flagship program, American Business Rescue, David helps CEOs, managers and entrepreneurs to get their businesses back on track. David builds on his experience as project manager for IBM, where, in his work with major clients such as Eastman Kodak and Ralph Lauren, he made IBM seventy million dollars using the same methodology he uses with consulting clients today. Over more than twenty years providing his insight, analysis and now coaching, David has a one hundred percent success rate.

David is also a coach and seminar trainer with New Peaks, the largest personal development training company in the world. He is a certified domain trading broker. He is the author of The Art of Traveling: Choreographing Your Best Trip Ever, *a book that merges his skill as a project manager with his passion for traveling. Connect with David at www.HibbsServices.com.*

Kip Brooks

MIRACLE CHILD

We named her Skylar Tianna. She was our miracle; she changed the world; and she only lived ninety-nine minutes.

On March 5, 2010, my wife Shannon and I went to an appointment for a 3-D ultrasound to find out the gender of our second child. We were bubbly, eager to see our baby. We were ecstatic to learn we were having a girl.

Our happiness was fleeting. That day Skylar was given an "unofficial diagnosis" of anencephaly, a rare birth defect that occurs when the brain fails to form completely.

"I'm sorry. This defect is fatal, and if she makes it to full-term, your daughter will not live long afterwards," the doctor explained.

The room went dark and everything began to shake. I had never felt so heavy or helpless. I couldn't hear anything except the loud pounding of my heart. I felt I was a huge failure because I had no answers. I thought, *I'm not strong enough for myself, much less my wife and son.* Shannon spoke to me the whole way home, but I couldn't tell you what she said. I was completely disconnected.

We discussed our options. Shannon was nineteen weeks pregnant, which meant that according to North Carolina state law, we had one week to decide if we would terminate the pregnancy before termination would no longer be an option. I was pretty sure

I wanted to terminate; going through with the pregnancy knowing our daughter would not live seemed like an unbearable burden for my wife, and we had a young son to consider. And yet, when I heard her heartbeat, it was as if a switch flipped.

By Friday, exactly one week after the diagnosis, we had decided two things: We would carry Skylar to term, enjoying every minute with her that we could, and we would become a donor family so

If she makes it to full-term, your daughter will not live long.

that another family could be saved the devastation we were feeling. If Skylar's life could not be saved, at least she could save the life of another child.

We quickly discovered that, due to a grey area in the donation laws, Skylar could not be an organ donor because of her particular diagnosis. The problem was, organ donors must be declared brain dead, but anencephalic infants don't meet that criterion, because they have at least partial brain stems. We also learned there was no protocol for children under age two to be donors. We decided to change that protocol.

I began contacting organ procurement organizations (OPOs), looking for options, looking for help. I sent out hundreds of emails and made almost as many phone calls; I contacted some of the OPOs many times. With every attempt, I was turned away.

Many of our friends and family members didn't understand our need to change this organ donation protocol and make it possible for other parents in our position to become donors, but we kept looking for a way. I was on a mission to "fix the system."

One day, four months after Skylar's diagnosis, I was sitting in a hotel room in Washington, D.C. when I received an email from one of the OPOs I had contacted more than once. The email essentially told me to stop bothering their small staff, that there was nothing they could do for us. They went on to say that, because they were spending so much time responding to my inquiries, they were losing valuable time in other, more productive areas. I was *crushed*. I felt as though I had failed at the only thing I could do.

I was confused; I was trying to help these OPOs fulfill their mission statements, but they were chasing me away. Hundreds had rejected me but this one cut me deeper than anything before or after. I broke down; staring at that computer screen, I began to accept that I had failed. We were only weeks away from Skylar's due date and, despite contacting any and every group I could think of, we hadn't gotten anywhere.

After wallowing in my tears for a few minutes I suddenly felt a switch inside, much as I had when I heard my daughter's heartbeat. I thought, *I'm allowing someone to take away the only thing I know*

**I felt as though I had failed at
the only thing I could do.**

---

for sure I am supposed to accomplish. I'm not going to let that happen. I started over again—emailing, calling and researching any case of organ donation involving young children I could find.

Then one day, I was walking through the parking lot after a terrible day at work, angrily mumbling under my breath, when my wife called. "A lady named Cynthia Willis, from LifeShare of the Carolinas just left our house. She found a way for Skylar to become a donor!"

I collapsed. I lost control and began sobbing tears of gratitude and relief. We had done it.

Cynthia, an organ donor coordinator for LifeShare of the Carolinas, explained that while we couldn't donate Skylar's organs, we could donate her liver cells to The Cytonet Group, an international biotechnology company with a location in Durham that processes cells for transplant or research.

Skylar lived for ninety-nine minutes. We were able to hold her and tell her how much we loved her. Our son Jadon was able to meet her and tell her how beautiful she was. Surrounded by family and friends, we spent every precious second with Skylar until she took her last breath, and we were at peace with our decision to bring her into the world.

Skylar's time on this planet was short, but our lives will never be the same. I now understand that when we aren't moving forward, going after what we know deep inside to be our purpose, we will automatically fall into a state of grief, a state of sorrow. We must stay in motion or our lives, our purposes, will become stagnant.

After a long process, we succeeded in having a protocol put in

Everyone wants their child to change the world. Our daughter did just that.

place to help families that want to donate in the infancy stage. Since her death, more than fifty families have been positively affected by her journey. My daughter's life also changed our lives in positive and unexpected ways. In Skylar's honor, Shannon started Seasons of Grief, a company dedicated to helping families of loss find healing.

As for me, I am forever altered by the experience. The transformative loss of Skylar, our miracle child, sparked a desire to be more and do more with my one, true, beautiful life. No parent should be tested by that fire, and yet it was in the profound pain of that experience that I earned the stripes of a leader, recognized the power of a father, and felt the fulfilling ability to make a difference in the lives of others. Everyone wants their child to change the world. Our daughter did just that.

Do not wait to take action toward something you want. We are born procrastinators and all too often end up running out of time way before we run out of hopes and dreams. When we stop denying our own mortality, we begin to live a more fulfilled life. If we had been unable to face Skylar's death, she may not have lived at all. In those short ninety-nine minutes, and in the months leading up to her birth, she made a difference.

What will you do with your time here? Will you leave this earth with regrets for the things you did not do, or memories of the experiences you had and the difference *you* made?

Kip Brooks is a Certified NLP (Neuro-linguistic Programming) Practitioner, coach, speaker, trainer and author. He works one-on-one and in teams to transform the hearts of former f#%k-ups, leaders and anyone who wants more, so that together, we might come to know our most extraordinary selves and transform the human experience on this planet.

Kip coaches and trains in a number of personal and business development areas, helping his clients learn how to be good husbands and providers, how to start a business, how to start over and how to change lives even with convictions and a drug history. Kip also coaches and trains on topics related to bereavement and the loss of a child: How to choose organ donation, telling your story in public, grieving in public and how to tell your story on national television.

A part of the John Maxwell Family, Kip is a certified trainer for the Maxwell Method. He is an active part of the Brendon Burchard Expert Academy trainings, is certified in T. Harv Eker's Train the Trainer program and an expert in the trainings of Steve Harrison, Jack Canfield and Bob Proctor.

In his book, Success Memoirs of a F#%k Up, *Kip details his early struggles, how he met the love of his life and the profound transformation he experienced after the death of his infant daughter, Skylar. To connect with Kip, visit www.KipBrooks.com.*

Laurel T. Colins

Your Beautiful Life

Your life is beautiful. Mired in the daily grind, focused on managing the stressful and ugly aspects of your life, you may not remember that you have a beautiful life, but you do. Your beautiful life exists. You don't have to search for it, or buy it or sacrifice for it. It's already yours. Living your beautiful life is as simple as recognizing you need to make a change.

In April of 2014, I lost my job. I was literally handed my walking papers, with the words "deleted" and "terminated" in bold. I was in shock and so angry. I couldn't believe someone I had worked so hard for, someone I had been so loyal *to,* could toss me aside so easily. Despite my inner turmoil, I was gracious when my boss handed me the papers. I thanked her and even hugged her; I didn't want her to think she got the better of me.

In the months that followed, my perfectly good life became an ugly one. I kept thinking: *Who am I? Am I no good? Why didn't my boss want me? I was so devoted to my job, so loyal to her, and worked so hard. I thought we were friends.* I was focused on the disappointment of losing my job, the betrayal, which began to affect my self-confidence and self-esteem. I lost my *joie de vivre.* Where did it go? I was looking everywhere for it.

When my former boss started telling a false story about why I left her company—that I had quit to start my own company—I was determined to tell the correct story. She fired me, and I had to go on unemployment insurance in order to support my children, and I wanted that truth to be known. I found myself living that story, telling people, "I don't have a job. I am on unemployment." I told this story over and over again, until it wasn't just my temporary circumstances, it was my identity. Who was this helping? Not me! It was undermining what little confidence I had left.

Eventually I realized I had suffered a trauma and that I needed professional help. I needed a complete life overhaul. It's hard to crawl back when you are thrown into an identity crisis and have to

My perfectly good life became an ugly one.

face an uncertain future, head on. And yet, somehow deep down in my heart, I knew my termination was an opportunity. I just had to stop fixating on the ugly story and write a new, beautiful story of my own choosing.

I went in search of guidance, mentorship and support, and found a new purpose. It started with baby steps. I looked for and celebrated the smallest victories. I practiced gratitude and started a journal, every night tracking the difference I made in someone else's life. I would reflect upon the day and think about any given moment when I felt most joyous—making a harried grocery store clerk laugh, finding an exquisite piece of furniture at a vintage shop, catching the last wisps of the sunset streaking across the sky.

As I tracked the simple pleasures of my day, the ugliness receded. I began to see a pattern, to see my own value and worth. I also noticed my interests and passions. I began to see what made me truly happy, and how to be the architect of my own beautiful life. In my search for inexpensive furnishings, I discovered and cultivated my innate ability to see beyond any imperfections to the beauty within. In second-hand pieces, I imagined the history; the gorgeous patina that was the ultimate result of time and abuse made them even more beautiful to me.

In the process of transforming my life from ugly back to beautiful, I created a unique system for redesigning a life, and set on a course to share that system with as many people as possible. I can say with total honesty, I am doing exactly what I love, and I find beauty in every day.

Beautiful living is about being honest with yourself and others; it is about forgiveness. It is living from the heart. Beautiful living is about joy and kindness, generosity and grace. Beautiful living is passion, and art, and dreams and creativity. It is your spirit and purpose, the unique value you bring to the world.

In your beautiful life, anything is possible and things will always get better. Anyone can feel this, experience this, *have* this. And you don't have to change jobs, or break relationships or take a dozen courses to do it. Your beautiful life is sitting there right beside your "ugly" one. You just have to open your eyes to the miracles in order to see them.

---

*Beautiful living is about being
honest with yourself and others.*

The key is to get into your own body and heart and to trust that you have the ability to tap into infinite possibilities. Set intentions for what you want in your life and keep those intentions and set reminders to yourself around your environments, with decor and vision boards. *Hold these intentions.* Be honest, because it must honestly be what you want, in your heart. Be helpful, because the more you help other people get what they want, the more chance you will have of getting what you want.

Be gracious and kind, and smile, and give compliments and put a good word out there, not an ugly complaining unappreciative word. Be grateful, because you have everything you need right now and if you can't appreciate what you have, then why would the universe send you more? Know that you will have challenges and may want to give up. You may be required to change course, but remember you can re-create and re-design your beautiful life and live the life you forgot you could dream.

There is power in your space, in your home and work environments. To live a beautiful life, you need a space that supports your dreams, helps you heal, inspires you to take action.

*It can take work every day to feel
like a beautiful person.*

You need a haven; your home needs to be a supportive space so that you can live harmoniously and reinforce intentions you have for your life.

In my seven-step system, I dedicate time to creating beautiful places in your home. The first step in my process you can do on your own. It involves doing a walkabout to observe the various areas of your home and determine if they support your life and needs. Your environments—and I mean *all* of them—dictate what you will do in them. When you want to make a change in your life, you need to change your environment.

For example, imagine you are single and want to attract a relationship. Do you have two comfortable chairs, or just one for you? Do you have a bed in the center of your bedroom with matching nightstands on either side? Do you have pictures of people or things in pairs, or pictures of people alone? The subconscious sees these things. Do you want the message to your subconscious to be that you are ready to welcome a new relationship, or that there is no room for anyone else in your space?

Perhaps you want to improve your health. As you walk about your space, take note. Is your kitchen clean? Do you enjoy going in there to make healthy food? Do you have fresh food or instant noodles? Is there old and mouldy food in the fridge? Is your pantry stocked with items that promote health? Do you sleep well? Is your bed comfortable? Are you using your bedroom part time as a TV room and an office and a fitness center? To transform your health, you need a clean kitchen well stocked with healthy food and the supplies and tools you need to make that food. You need a bedroom that is designed as a space for rest, rejuvenation and intimacy.

It is a very personal thing; everyone has different needs from their environments. But we all need to take a look at all of our spaces to see if the environment and the items in it are giving us energy or depleting it. If you are coming home every day and looking at a vase your ex-partner gave you and you are not on good terms, you feel angry every time you look at it. Does it matter that the vase is expensive, that it was the only gift they ever gave you, or even that you like it? No. Get rid of it.

Your subconscious mind processes emotional attachments in a split second, and as you move through your space your brain is madly assessing and processing everything. And you wonder why you are overwhelmed and exhausted? Keep only the things that inspire you and send good and appropriate messages to your subconscious, messages that support and reinforce the happiness and joy you want in your beautiful life.

You can live a beautiful life right now, but it can take work every day to feel like a beautiful person. You don't just clear clutter once just as you don't make a deposit into your savings account once. You must create a practice of making beautiful, honest, gracious choices with your beautiful life. I practise every day to maintain and expand and grow the beauty of my life. The more I become unconsciously competent with my daily practice, the more I am able to share and help others to create their own.

The very first step is taking responsibility for your life. You may not have been responsible for the wounds or life events that formed the person you are now and the life you live currently, but you are responsible for making the commitment to move past them. Forgive the past and the people who were a part of the ugly story you have been telling yourself.

You are the one who allows yourself to not feel of value, and it is just as easy to tell yourself you are worthy as it is to tell yourself that you are not. Accept the responsibility that you are the one who allows the story to continue and know that you have the power to tell a new story: the new story of your fabulous, bold and beautiful life.

Your beautiful life begins now.

Laurel T. Colins is "The Beautiful Living Coach" from beautiful Nelson, B.C. As a decorator, stylist, color expert and feng shui consultant, Laurel has an innate ability to create beautiful and nurturing environments, which support and empower people to live their best lives. As a beautiful living coach, Laurel works with people to get crystal clear on their goals and to create strategies to achieve them. Her expertise lies in her ability to communicate with clients, interpret their needs and assist them in bringing beauty, ease, elegance, organization, joy and style into their lives.

Laurel is an alumna of The Western School of Feng Shui in California, is a Maria Killiam trained true color expert, and was personally trained in dream coach methodology by Marcia Wieder of Dream University. Connect with Laurel at www.TheBeautifulLivingCoach.com.

Catherine Blanchette-Dallaire

A New Story

A six-year-old boy waits on the porch of his house. Today is his birthday. He is turning six. The party goes on in the house, but he is waiting outside, alone. He is waiting for his father to show up, which will never happen.

This story seems harmless, but this specific moment will have an impact on the little boy's entire life, and not on a positive way.

When the little boy understands that his father isn't coming, a switch occurs inside his heart. Unable to explain why his father is away on the day of his birthday, the boy will choose the most evident reason: His father doesn't like him. A monstrous hole forms in the boy's heart and feelings of emptiness, uselessness and loneliness rush in to fill it.

The little boy will never be the same. Convinced his father doesn't care for him, the boy will do everything he can to make his father love him again. He will stay on this quest for years, but over time, he will forget the purpose. The deep emotions filling the hole in his heart will remain, influencing his relationships. He will do whatever it takes to feel loved, and this from the first person willing to pay attention to him. He will lose himself one piece at a time trying to get his father's love back. He will do things he normally would not do, say things he normally would not say and accept things he normally would not accept, ultimately becoming someone he would not normally become.

Chances are, the little boy will never get his father's love back, because he is looking neither in the right direction nor at the right time. When he enters relationships, he is not looking for love with that person, but for love from his father. He is not seeking at the right time, because his adult self does not miss love; it is the six-year-old boy inside of him. This is why he may never fill up the hole he feels inside.

Most of our fears belong to the past.

Most of our fears belong to the past. Not only because the person or the thing that created this fear lives in the past tense, but also because that fear lives in a past version of us. Often, past fears live in our inner child, a zero- to ten-year-old version of us.

For example, a little boy who once disappointed his parents may fear failure all his life. A little girl who was abused by one man may fear all men as an adult. A little boy who did not feel his father's approval may find approval in the arms of many women. A little girl who once stayed stuck in an igloo may fear black and closed areas a long time afterward. A little boy who assumed he wasn't good enough for his father may become a workaholic trying to be good enough for everyone. All of these behaviours are only placebos trying to calm the turmoil in our inner child's heart. But the more we keep using the placebo, the less we work on the real cause of our fears and pain.

I share this with you because I've been there and done that. I've sought my father's love in men's arms; I've sought my parents' approval in my friends' and boss's eyes, saying yes to all their requests. I went on an impossible quest to be loved and appreciated—impossible because I could never get enough. The holes in my heart emptied as fast as I put love from others into them, because I was filling them with the wrong love, at the wrong time.

I lived that way for a long time, until the day it all exploded.

I was twenty-three. I was dating a happy guy, the kind of person who seems to never have any problems and to be in total control of his life. Through him I felt happiness for the first time of my life… until he dumped me on a street corner.

That moment was my spark. *How can he be so happy? So free? So himself?* I thought he was egocentric. I was mad at him for being himself. He wasn't concerned with the opinions of others, whereas I was living by and for the opinion of others. He was allowing himself to be; I was acting according to what other people demanded, or what I thought they wanted. He was saying, 'no;' I was the best servant anyone could hope for.

Life was good to him; why was it so cruel to me? He was happy, and yet I had learned that happiness was not something I could reach for, because I was not worthy. I believed I didn't have the *right* to access happiness.

I had absolutely no clue who I really was.

As time passed, I finally realized that all of my resentment toward my ex-boyfriend was actually directed toward me, because *I* was the person who was not allowing myself to be. My whole life was a lie.

I had been lying to myself and to others. From that point on I knew I could never reconnect with my past, but I had no clue that a change was possible, so I was lost in an emotional "No Man's Land." My pain was loud and deep. I was completely lost. *Life isn't worth living*, I thought, and contemplated suicide. *I don't have any reasons to stay alive in this life of duty.*

Then, a little voice inside me spoke up for the first time. It said, "Leave the country and start all over again on the other side of the earth." I felt such a release at the thought of starting over. I decided to plan on doing it, but very quickly realized the plan was only an escape. My "duty" mode would follow me where I went. I asked myself, *Why does moving overseas sound so great to me? Why can*

I find a reason to live abroad but not here in Québec? Why would I be worthy in another country, but not here?

Again, I realized something vital: Escape was not a solution, but a Band-Aid on a problem. I would have to face my actual world and make changes here before anything else. I started to cry big

---

If you want to live your life in the present with a free mind and body, start to clean your past.

---

heaving sobs. So much emotion poured out of me: anger, fear, loneliness, powerlessness and pain. I thought it would never end.

Then, on June first of 2006, I got caught in a massive thunderstorm while out walking. The winds were strong as I walked soaked to the bone; my running shoes were heavy with water. I did not run home or seek shelter. Instead I let nature wash my whole body and mind. I felt happy, as if I was truly breathing for the first time in my life. There in the storm I thought, *I feel good here and now. I have a place in this world. I am worthy.*

From that point on, I began my biggest challenge: rebuilding my life and freeing myself from past injuries, stories and pain. *I will stop living in the past and learn to live in the present.*

Because I used to live a silent life of obedience, I had absolutely no clue who I really was. I asked myself, "What do I like? Who am I? What are my strengths? What are my qualities? What is my favorite color? What kind of music motivates me? What kind of job would I like to do? What kind of men do I like?"

Then I asked myself, "What do I dislike? What don't I want anymore? What are my boundaries? Do I have any boundaries at all? How can I express myself? What will happen if I say 'no' to someone or something?"

As I practiced allowing myself to be me, I faced my family, my friends and my boss with a new freedom, new possibilities, new desires, new rights. I had to learn how to say 'no' and possibly disappoint people, how to be intimate with someone, how to express my needs with no fear of judgment and ask for what I wanted. I rewound my life and took time to look at my past and see it through my "new pair of glasses."

It took me years to understand a fundamental fact: All my actual fears were fears of past events, not present ones. I feared life when I was young, but I do not need to fear life now. I missed love when I was young, but I am not missing love today. My needs were unfulfilled when I was seven years old, but today I am enough strong to fulfill them myself. I did not have the possibility to be me as a young child, but only I can stop myself from living authentically now. I realized, *My inner child may be broken, but the grown-up me has the capacity to learn the tools to be happy.*

Any small event you lived at a younger age truly affects the way you interact with life and the way you live your fears. But you can stop this. You can change this if you allow your inner child to reconnect with this broken part of yourself, allowing the grown-up you to love, care and help your inner child solve his or her issues. Release from past fears is possible, but it requires you to be willing and open to start a long journey into your past.

If you want to live your life in the present with a free mind and body, start to clean your past. Understand how many holes you have in your own heart, to which situation they belong, to whom they refer, and how your inner child reacted. At that age, you neither had the tools, the comprehension nor the vision to understand the meaning of these moments. But now you have them or can learn them. You can now teach these tools to your mini-me, helping him or her to understand and see things differently. After all, maybe the father of the little six-year-old boy in the story never stopped loving his son. Perhaps he was simply stuck at work, or in traffic.

To begin your journey to cleaning your past, list ten of your fears. Then, look back on your childhood and find two events that could tie back to most of your fears. Which of these two events creates the strongest reaction in you? Reconnect with that event. Try to imagine a different scenario and outcome. Imagine the event playing out the way you would have loved it to happen; explore the infinite sides of the penny. Allow yourself to release this event and be you. This fear no longer has a place in your mind or your body. Live your own life now, the one you choose, the one that is perfect for your grown-up self.

Releasing the past also allow you to better connect with your inner voice, which is the expression of your heart and your higher self, the part of you that is pure and not changed or violated or influenced by past events. If you used to think that your little voice was saying crazy things your fears could not allow you to trust, releasing the past allows that voice to speak more freely and helps you make heart-centered choices that become the main steppingstones of a clear path to any best future you choose to be yours.

You cannot erase the past but you can for sure close the book on it and start a new story, a new story with any happy ending you want. How will your new story begin?

Catherine Blanchette-Dallaire is an author, speaker and life coach. Her mission is to assist people and provide tools they can use to release fears, pain and traumas from their past and live their present life, the way they deserve it, with free mind and body. Over the course of several years, Catherine developed a trauma release technique she used to free herself from her childhood pain and imprints. Strong and effective, this technique makes a huge difference in her clients' lives. She also teaches seminars on fear management.

In 2012 Catherine broke both of her ankles in a sports accident and lived four months in a wheelchair. She used this experience to found OnRoule (www.OnRoule.org), a social project connecting people with reduced mobility with accessible commerce, resources, activities and housing in order to live an easier life with no boundaries. For her work with OnRoule, Catherine has received many awards.

Catherine is the author of the forthcoming book Learn to Dance With Your Fears and Reach Your Goals: Seven Easy Steps to Move Forward and Live with Free Mind and Body. *Connect with Catherine at www.farendole.ca.*

Douglas C. Curtiss, MD

A BRILLIANT FUTURE

In the introduction to our book, *Dyslexic AND UN-Stoppable*, my wife Lucie wrote, "You've been given an exceptional gift. It's your chance to make this world a better place." This is not typically how dyslexics—or their families—perceive dyslexia when it is first identified. Some may never come to realize this and instead buy into the belief that there is something wrong with them, letting dyslexia hinder them and keep them from their greatness.

We all have a unique set of talents, and our authentic success depends not on our ability to overcome the challenges and circumstances we experience, but on how we embrace these challenges and circumstances as gifts and succeed *because* of them. Helping dyslexics discover their inner power and create a brilliant future is our mission. This is our story.

When our son Félix-Alexander (we call him FéZander) was a toddler and in pre-school, he was smart and inquisitive. He seemed to learn quickly and always wanted to know how things worked. He was—and still is—a caring and engaged student. In kindergarten, FéZander's report cards described him as "developing appropriately," but they also stated that he read below his grade level. He loved having books read to him and enjoyed discussing the story, yet when he sat down to read himself he found it to be incredibly laborious.

In first grade, teachers described him as one of the best students they'd ever had. One teacher said, "Thank you for sharing him with us. He's awesome."

They said he was curious, creative and caring. He was respectful of the teachers and persistent in his attempts to complete lessons. FéZander loved math and science, and as long as he received instructions verbally, he excelled. Yet written instructions seemed to be challenging for him. When reading books, he would look at the pictures first and then the text. He would often grow tired of reading and then resist learning altogether.

We noticed other children in FéZander's class progressing to longer and more complex books, and yet he continued to struggle with the easiest books. At the same time, we realized our daughter, Chloé, who is twenty-one months younger than our son, was an advanced reader. She started reading at age three and was finishing chapter books at four.

One day, I was sitting with FéZander helping him with his homework. Despite my efforts, he just wasn't "getting it." He began to squirm in his chair, then shift the focus to talk about

He would often grow tired of reading
and then resist learning altogether.

unrelated topics, and then shift again to try to do something else. I became so frustrated I slammed my first on the table and yelled, "Concentrate!" Of course he just shut down.

Later that day, reflecting on my actions, I felt ashamed—ashamed that I had lost my temper and ashamed because I was a Yale-trained pediatrician who was supposed to know everything and I still couldn't help my son. I was stressed and worried that the situation was hopeless. I didn't know where to turn.

At the end of first grade, we met with our son's teachers. They said, "We recommend FéZander repeat first grade. His reading is not up to grade level."

In my mind I heard the voices of my patients who, years later, were still traumatized by repeating first grade. I wished someone could see the brilliance I saw in my son and could offer us real answers.

Lucie and I immediately said, "No!" We knew repeating a grade was not the answer, so we made a commitment: We would do anything to get him the help he needed. Although Lucie had discovered she was dyslexic in her twenties, and there were definitely clues that Fezander was dyslexic, we weren't sure he was.

We knew repeating a grade was not the answer.

We enrolled him in a remedial reading program. After two months, we realized this program wasn't working. We later learned this was because it was geared toward students who simply have to catch up and English as a Second Language students, not toward our son's reading challenges.

Through much searching and trying different schools, courses and online resources, we found a specialized school for dyslexic children. After two months at the school, FéZander went from reading at a kindergarten level to a second-grade level. We began to realize he was, in fact, dyslexic. After four years of one-on-one instruction after his regular school—twice a week during the school year and twenty sessions every summer—FéZander finished his work there and is now excelling in school.

Not everyone is as lucky as FéZander. Lucie and I saw friends whose children were struggling with similar issues—decoding words, reading, spelling, grammar, following written instructions—and were put into special education. These children barely progressed. More and more my patients spoke to me about the trauma of being held back in school. I knew some parents could not afford the private tutoring we provided for our son. I was so grateful to see our son begin to build his own brilliant future, I wanted the same for these kids. What could we do to help?

Lucie and I had participated in personal development courses over the years, and I had signed on with a coach who wanted me to establish an online presence as a pediatrician. I had tried that before, but nothing came of it.

I said to Lucie, "What would I do, anyway?"

We had no idea.

We took the challenge of dyslexia
and transformed it into a gift.

Then one day, the answer came to Lucie in a flash. Our commute to our kids' school is thirty to forty minutes each way. On the drive to pick the kids up from school, she thought about growing up in the 1970s, unaware that she had dyslexia. She thought about her struggles and our son's journey, and how through her knowledge and experience with dyslexia, she was able to help him. She started connecting the dots—her story, his story, my scientific and experiential knowledge as a pediatrician.

When she came home she said, "I know what we're going to do. We are going to help all of those dyslexic kids and adults out there who can't afford special schools, or can't get access to them. We're going to write a book about our story."

Lucie wrote *Dyslexic AND UN-Stoppable* to give parents of dyslexic children real hope as well as the tools and strategies they need to help their kids create their own brilliant future. I contributed the question and answer section using the questions I had been asked by patients over the past eighteen years as a pediatrician. To make it interactive and useful to busy parents, we integrated the book with our website, offering videos demonstrating our tools and strategies. We also wrote a companion cookbook sharing recipes based on the nutritional support we gave our son that helped him increase brain power, focus and concentration.

We took the challenge of dyslexia and transformed it into a gift. Then, we worked hard to give that gift to the world. We preach persistence and we teach kids to be unstoppable and we are learning this ourselves from this process. Though we did not self-publish our books, we still had a remarkable amount of work to do to get the word out. At times we were frustrated, getting "no" after "no" from bookstores who would not stock our books on their shelves.

But when we are discouraged, we remember the kids who need us. If we don't reach them, they will flounder. We remember that, according to the International Dyslexia Association, fifteen to twenty percent of the population has some symptom of dyslexia. We remember that, according to the *Denver Post,* more than fifty percent of prison inmates are dyslexic. And we remember the promise of every child, the dreams that could go unfulfilled, the amazing contributions that might never happen, the bright futures that could be dimmed if children do not receive the help they need.

We reconnect to the why, to the purpose of our mission. And we reconnect to our son's triumph. Today, FéZander is at the top of his class. He reads tons of books—last summer he was reading a book my mother was reading. To see him come from barely able to do anything related to reading or writing in first grade to excelling in every subject, happy and eager to learn, we know what's possible.

We were able to intervene before our son gave up. The drive to help other precious souls before life and difficult people squash them down keeps us going. If it takes more work to get our books out in the world, I don't care. One way or another, our message will be received: In every seemingly hopeless situation, there is an answer. In every challenge, there is a gift we are meant to share with the world. And in every child, there is an unstoppable spirit, a beautiful dream and a brilliant future.

Douglas C. Curtiss, MD, FAAP is a Yale-trained pediatrician and a very left-brained thinker. He is also the husband of a dyslexic and the father of a dyslexic. Having seen the amazing success of his son in overcoming dyslexia, and using it to create a fantastic life, Doug was struck by the contrast with some of the children in his pediatric practice who struggle with dyslexia, not knowing where to turn. As a result, Doug teamed up with his wife to help all parents and kids with dyslexia find the tools and strategies to have a brilliant future.

With his wife Lucie Curtiss, a pediatric nurse, Doug wrote the book Dyslexic AND UN-Stoppable: How Dyslexia Helps Us Create the Life of Our Dreams and How You Can Do It Too *and the companion cookbook,* Dyslexic AND UN-Stoppable The Cookbook: Revealing Our Secrets How Having Healthier Brains and Lifestyles Helps Us Overcome Dyslexia. *Connect with Doug at www. DyslexicAndUnstoppable.com.*

Edit Faris

Put on Your Own Mask First

If you've ever flown on a plane, you know the pre-flight safety demonstration includes instructions about what to do when the cabin loses oxygen: Put on your own mask first and then help your child or other people next to you. The reason behind this is simple. If you help others first, you may pass out from lack of oxygen before you get your own mask on. If, on the other hand, you have your mask firmly in place, you can help anyone who needs it.

Now, if you've ever read a self-help book, you've probably also heard the "life mask" analogy applied to advice about self-care. It makes sense. When you hear it, you nod your head in agreement and take notes. Maybe you even underline the part about focusing on yourself first, because you know that you focus on everyone else first, and wouldn't your life be amazing if you practiced self-care and followed your heart first for once?

It's not that simple, though, is it? So often, we realize we need to take better care of ourselves—our bodies, our hearts, our minds, our inner child, our first dreams—and then do little or nothing about it, opting instead to take care of everyone else's needs *first*. As the flight attendants tell us, that means we never get around to our stuff. We can't. We didn't put on the mask, first.

For me, realizing I needed to make big changes and start focusing on my own needs was a slow process. It started about three years ago. Married with three children, a home to attend to and a cake decorating business to run, I was caught up in the business and stress of life. I had no idea how to create balance in my life and did everything out of duty to my family or my business, never pausing to regenerate, to dream, to plan or get clarity. At the time, I didn't even know that I was *supposed* to think about any of that!

I started to notice that every morning I woke up feeling depressed, as if the life was sucked out of me. I remembered the excitement, joy and passion I had when I was seventeen. I longed

I had no idea how to create balance in my life.

for that feeling and for the girl I was at that age, when I could still dream and believed whatever I dreamt up was entirely possible.

In 2012, while at a bakery convention, I met a business coach who changed my entire world. Through working with him, I discovered what taking full responsibility for my life really meant. He said, "Your business will only grow as much as you are willing to grow, learn and change." I was excited; learning was never a problem for me. I was ready to grow, but I still didn't know how to do that.

Through my coach I discovered and rediscovered some of the great thought leaders of our century: Zig Ziglar, Bryan Tracey, Napoleon Hill, Jim Rhon. It was Jim Rhon who said, "Work harder on yourself than you do on your job." Reading that quote opened my mind; it was the first time I considered the fact that my success was directly related to how much energy and time I focused on myself, not my business.

I started thinking about happiness—what it meant, what would make me happy. Would I be happy if I was rich? Would I be happy if I did not have my marriage? I came to understand that happiness is a choice, and only I have the power to make myself happy. That was huge for me. I had been taking action, but it wasn't *inspired* action. I told myself, "It's time to find out what you really want from life and trust your inner voice to guide you."

I began to rediscover *me*. I found the courage to become me again, to do the things that made *me* happy. I reconnected to what I was passionate about and began to trust my inner guiding voice. I made it a part of my morning routine to journal and visualize the future outcome. I used affirmations about myself and about different areas of my life that needed immediate transformation: health, diet, business, relationships. I made little flashcards that I carried in my purse and, when doubt set in, I pulled them out to lift my spirit.

Then, I began to take stock and face the hard realities. Looking around at my beautiful storefront bakery, which I designed myself, I realized that my heart was not in the business. It wasn't that I didn't want to bake beautiful special events cakes for my clients anymore; I just didn't want the grind of maintaining a store. My

Everything started to flow easily.

children missed me when I was at work, and I wanted to be there for them. But how could I give up the dream of owning a bakery, when I had worked so hard to see it to fruition?

Talking it over with my husband, I realized I didn't have to give up my business. Instead, I could just give up the storefront. I had three years left on my lease, so the change might be difficult—and expensive. I had a lot of fear around making the decision. But the more I thought about it, the more optimistic I became. Finally, I decided to let go of the storefront.

I felt instant relief after making the decision. Suddenly, I was happier. I felt lighter. Everything started to flow easily, and it seemed as if time sped up, bringing me one positive outcome after another. My landlord was very supportive and understanding; he let me out of my lease without an issue. Our existing customers had no issue with doing business with a home-based cake business and continued their support. They were even willing to pay my increased prices, probably because I was now able to give them more personal attention.

Within less than two weeks after we announced we were closing, I moved out of the storefront and was up and running at my house. With a huge part of my overhead eliminated, I was able to take on sophisticated orders that required more of my time. As a result, I achieved higher profits with fewer orders.

As I poured the beautifully mixed, smooth batter into cake pans, I felt the rush of satisfaction and pleasure I used to feel when I baked. The sight of the silky, billowy buttercream that made all of our customers rave about our products made me smile with pride.

Put your own life mask on—today.

The sunshine streaming through my kitchen window as I worked in rhythmic motion made me feel at peace. And the happiness on my children's faces when they realized I would really be there for them when they needed me was worth everything. I was truly free.

During this time, I also came to another painful decision. Throughout the process of letting go of the storefront, I realized our marriage was no longer serving our growth. Still, it took me a long time to get the courage to tell my husband how I felt. We had three children and an "average" marriage—why would someone want to leave? And yet, as I rediscovered my true self I also transformed my beliefs about having to stay in a relationship out of duty.

Finally, I found the courage to talk to my husband about my feelings. I said, "Please be open, and try to understand what I went through and accept my friendship. I still love you, but this is a different kind of love, a love that accepts and respects you. It is a love that wants you to be happy and find your own way. It is a love that is supportive. We will always have a connection because of our children, it's just that now, that expression of love will change."

Because I came to him from a place of love, acceptance and respect, I got the same back from him. He now sees and understands my vision for the future and supports me in my endeavors. I also support him with *his* plans to start over and engage in a new business. Because we skipped the drama and fights, our children hardly noticed that we divorced.

Before I took full responsibility for the creation of every moment of my life, I felt overwhelmed. I was so busy working in my business, I totally burned myself out. I didn't have time to focus on my own basic needs, to think, to get clarity, to recover and spend time on things that could create a difference in my life. I got caught up in the doing, doing, doing and always trying to control the outcome.

Coaching myself out of this "swimming against the current" state made room for opportunities, people and events to show up in my life. My actions became inspired actions. Some days I still have long, hard days, but my energy is different: *it's happy.*

When I put the life mask on myself for the first time, everything in my life changed for the better. Now, I put it on every day, first thing. This means I sleep enough; I've improved my health, energy and focus, which has made me more creative, productive and patient. My children are happy, because I spend more time with them. I pay attention to what I create through my thoughts and feelings.

Today, the view from my office is my beautiful, green backyard. I turn on the music and sing and dance to the rhythm as the sunshine streams in. I treat myself with more compassion and gentleness and I forgive myself when I make a mistake, all of which enables me to see others with compassion. Hurts that used to take a long time to heal disappear in a short time or never occur anymore. My changed inner world attracts different kinds of people and situations into my life, and I am grateful for them.

Put your own life mask on—today. Begin the process to reconnect to your heart, to the joyful child within you, and find your own happiness. Gain clarity about what you want out of life, why you want it and how you want to feel when you are there. Make sure the life you live is yours and not somebody else's expectation for you. Find your passion and take steps toward it, no matter how small the steps are.

Put the mask on. You deserve to be happy. You deserve to live.

Edit Faris is a certified Law of Attraction Life Coach and ActionCoach Business Coaching franchise owner, whose mission is to inspire women to find their own power and inner strength by returning to their true selves. Through her company, Powerhouse Coaching and Consulting, LLC, she provides business and life coaching services, as well as workshops to help her clients continue to grow, accept and honor themselves. Using tools from her training and education, as well her own personal experience transforming her own life, Edit helps clients achieve joy and fulfillment with gratitude and playfulness, while cultivating their feminine energy and commitment to their own happiness. She is also passionate about changing lives through helping her clients create and grow their businesses, which enables them to contribute to economic growth and create jobs and more abundance in our country.

Edit is also is the owner of Dream Cakes, Inc., a special-event cake company specializing in gorgeous and delicious wedding cakes, cupcakes and pastries custom made for clients. A self-taught baker and cake designer, her ambitions started in her grandmother's kitchen as a little girl in Hungary. Reading and dreaming about exotic ingredients and flavors ignited her passion for the culinary arts. Connect with Edit at www.DreamCakesInc.com and at www.ActionCoach.com/ EditFaris.

Timothy Lafolette

ONE SMALL CHANGE

To a person who is not depressed, most of the thoughts and feelings I'll describe in this story are so completely foreign they seem unfathomable. In retrospect, I feel foolish for having wasted so much time in that sort of emotional and mental state. However, I realize that these experiences served to help me understand depression first-hand and how to work through it. Now, I can listen to clients, hear their stories and offer them deep understanding and compassion, because I've been there too.

Standing on the stage with my cast-mates, the lights blur my view of the audience. Years of performing in the chorus of various theatrical productions has prepared me well for this moment, standing out front in a leading role. It is a stretch for me—so many lines, so much music to learn. Yet, as I step forward and sing the iconic song everyone recognizes, I let the lyrics wash over me and my nerves subside. *I know this song. I know this journey. I know this truth.*

I remember the day we first rehearsed "Seasons of Love" from the Tony award-winning Broadway musical *Rent*. Like most people, I had a vague recollection of the song; it is often performed at graduations and other school performances. We worked on the song for almost the entire rehearsal to get a good feel for it and to look at it lyrically and musically, adding different layers.

As the practice came to an end, I realized the main message of the song is the message most therapists focus on: Measure your life in positive moments, not in the negative or the mundane. Measure your life not in bad things that happened in the past, or worries about the future; instead, measure it in happiness and joy, in staying together, in friendship. "Measure in love…"

I wasn't always able to measure my life in positive moments. My family loved and cared about me, and yet from the age of twelve I started experiencing some depressive symptoms and suicidal

---

I started experiencing some depressive symptoms and suicidal thoughts.

---

thoughts. I couldn't act on them because I was raised in a home with strong religious beliefs and the understanding that suicide was wrong and that I would go to hell for it. Instead, I prayed fervently, "Please let me die in my sleep."

I couldn't control the thoughts and I couldn't force myself to feel better. It wasn't that my life was horrible or that I had experienced an unbearable trauma; I just didn't want to wakeup to face the next day. It wasn't all of the time; some days everything seemed okay. Most of the time, though, I was faking it—I felt depressed inside and tried to make everything on the outside *appear* to be okay.

My thoughts frequently focused on the resources spent on me—what it cost to clothe me, feed me, shelter me, educate me. I told myself, "You don't deserve it. Those resources would be better spent on someone else." I was convinced that if I died, someone of value would get my "share" of resources, the share I was not worthy of receiving.

Despite how I felt, I never missed a day of school or work due to my depression. This isn't always the case for people who deal with depression, who often have trouble functioning and completing day-to-day tasks. This is also why my depression went unnoticed by the people who loved me. I appeared to be just like any other kid who had good days and bad days. No one knew the truth, or how severe the situation really was.

I didn't enjoy much of anything, but I tried to hang on to anything that mildly interested me, like eating or listening to music. I enjoyed theatre and music and performing, and for brief moments in rehearsal and on stage I forgot about the emptiness I felt inside. Obligations to others saved my life over and over again. If I was in a play or musical I would tell myself, "Just wait until the run is over, until you've fulfilled your commitment to your cast-mates." The primary reason I didn't kill myself was I didn't want to hurt anyone who cared about me.

My depression remained through high school and into college. In nursing school, I decided to see the therapist at the student health clinic. The service was included in our healthcare coverage, and since I planned to enter the mental health field, I wanted to see what therapy was like. This decision, this one small change, was the beginning of a new life for me.

With the help of my therapist I got clarity about my depression and started to see the positive possibilities for my life, using tools like keeping a gratefulness journal. But it wasn't an overnight change—nothing like the movies! My depression lifted slowly over time, as I made a series of shifts in thought. I started to let go of

---

I didn't enjoy much of anything.

---

the feelings of unworthiness and to see my life as useful, enjoyable, purposeful. I began to accept who I was—depressive feelings and all—and stopped trying to be what I perceived everyone wanted me to be.

As the song "Seasons of Love" suggests, I stopped measuring my life in negative things and started focusing on the good experiences I had had and the positive aspects of my life, and this shifted my perspective. As I looked at the world and myself with a different perspective, I started to *feel* differently about the world and my place in it.

Transformation—whether you are living with a mental illness or trying to reinvent yourself—is not about making big changes all at once. It's about the one small change that makes all the difference, the change that puts you on a new path and makes your life that much better. Slow, steady, incremental change will get you on the right path, but remember, you've never truly arrived somewhere.

You are constantly learning, growing and changing, constantly starting new chapters and seasons, and sometimes that means dealing with familiar challenges. After I first felt my depressive symptoms and suicidal thoughts had begun to subside, they came back full force, sneaking up on me not long after I finished my

---

*There is always someone who
is qualified to help you.*

---

nurse practitioner program and started working. The reality of how much school debt I was in compared to how much I was earning triggered those old feelings of not being worth the resources "spent" on me, and I started planning my suicide.

After years of medical training, I knew exactly how to pull it off and I had it planned to the letter. But there was another difference this time around: I had tools to deal with these thoughts. Once again, it began with one small change. I returned to my gratitude journal, a method I had used in the early part of my recovery and had set aside when I got busy with school and work. Every day I jotted down answers to simple questions: What went right today? What tiny thing am I thankful for? What surprised me today? What positive thoughts did I have today?

I began to measure my life in love, wherever I could see it, in every little beautiful thing. Gratitude is powerful. If you can focus on one or two things to be grateful for in a situation, it can really start to turn things around. Or, at the very least, it can neutralize an otherwise negative situation.

Eventually, the suicidal thoughts subsided again and the depressive symptoms lifted. Later, I would attend the "Millionaire Mind Intensive," which helped me realize I could use some of the same principles for my mental health to help with my finances and career. These habits made a big difference in how I felt about myself as well as my financial picture.

Our thoughts are powerful, and yet most of us pay little attention to them. Sometimes life is really difficult, and old thoughts come back up. I'll hear myself saying, "I can't do this" or "I really don't want to wake up tomorrow morning and face life," but now it takes less effort for me to recognize that these are not rational thoughts and to remind myself that I have faced similar or greater challenges before and come out okay.

One small mental shift can make such a difference, but it's not as though if you make this one small change you will be good for the rest of your life. You make this decision every day. Sometimes you will find yourself falling back into old patterns, but if you can remind yourself that you *are* falling back, and that you have the tools to overcome, it's easier to get back on track faster.

As a psychiatric mental health nurse practitioner, I work with clients who are living with addiction. It is common for them to relapse, but what I've noticed is, after they relapse, they come back even more determined to stay clean and sober. It's not the relapse, but how they respond to the relapse. Succeeding in making any transformation is about how you react when you falter. Do you forgive yourself quickly and move on, or do you sit there and beat yourself up over it? It's easy to choose shame and guilt because that's where we naturally go when we make mistakes, or when we go back to something that isn't right for us.

As I tell my clients, "You're here now. You're doing it right now. Today is a different day, and today you are making a different choice."

Many of my clients have gone through a dozen different drug and alcohol programs. They've tried to work the twelve steps; they've done all of the things you would expect somebody who is trying to get clean to do. They ask me, "Why isn't this working?" Drug and alcohol counselors always say—and I support this, too—"What is the one thing you are doing differently?"

A lot of times my clients realize they do have some mental health challenges that are making it harder to stay clean and sober. So, now they are seeing me to address their mental health, which they have not really paid attention to in the past. I usually remind them, "Addressing your mental health *is* the one thing you're doing differently."

We collaborate about their mental health treatment, which may include medications, and work together to make sure that the plan is working well for them. This, in combination with talk therapy with a therapist and working on their drug and alcohol treatment, brings them to a healthier place where they are able to maintain housing, a job and their sobriety over time. In essence, they have a new lease on life. They don't have to make the same old decisions and they feel empowered to move forward.

It's important to remember that you are not alone. No matter what you're going through, there is always someone who is qualified to help you, who *wants* to help you. If you are living with mental health or emotional issues, don't give up too soon. There are many treatment options available to you: talk therapy, medication, over-the-counter supplements, herbal treatments, yoga, exercise, diet, meditation, EFT/tapping, acupuncture, NLP, biofeedback and the list goes on.

If you're not struggling with mental health, but have other things that need improvement, there is still someone who has a similar issue and has figured out one way of dealing with it. So, ask for help. Start learning more so you are better able to address your issue, whatever it is.

Make one small change. Begin with a shift in perspective. Measure your life in different ways. Rather than keep track of all you should have done, all the mistakes you've made, or all of the negative experiences you've had, count the positives. Rather than stack up all of the obstacles, count your unique advantages, resources and supporters. Rather than measure in doubt, fear or regret, measure in laughter, in simple pleasures, in joy. *Measure in love.*

Timothy Lafolette is a psychiatric mental health nurse practitioner and Psychiatric Services Manager at NARA NW (Native American Rehabilitation Association) in Portland, Oregon. He attended Oregon Health and Sciences University in Portland for his nursing education, and George Fox University in Newberg, Oregon for his undergraduate degree. Timothy also sings in the Portland Opera Chorus on a regular basis and has participated in numerous productions of community theater in the greater Portland area. He grew up in San Francisco, but went to high school in Hermiston, Oregon, a rural, agricultural town, providing him with a different perspective of country versus city living. He is honored and grateful to be a part of this book project.

Chelsea Markel

GRATITUDE IS THE KEY

I love my life.

This powerful mantra has completely transformed my life. This statement has beome the most important part of my day, as I find myself creating space for gratitude, thankfulness and inner peace.

The practice of creating space for gratitude and thankfulness has changed my life in the most beautiful way. It's through my experience with gratitude that I have been able to take my coaching practice across the world with just word of mouth marketing, and it's why my life is filled with witnessing the transformations and breakthroughs of others. I'm blessed to work for a company that trains millions of people across the globe in how to live a more peaceful, prosperous and fulfilling life. This company is New Peaks™, which has become my sanctuary for growth, learning and community.

I'm blessed. I'm grateful to say that my dad is CEO of New Peaks™ (formerly Peak Potentials). By the age of sixteen, I was fortunate enough to experience the teachings and practices of this company and this kick-started my passion and excitement for this business. From the time I was a little girl, I wanted to make a difference in the world.

What I learned from my father and from the brilliant thought leaders I met and read and trained with gave me the confidence to move forward in pursuit of my dreams at a very young age. I started my coaching practice when I was still in high school; I was sixteen years old. I had just won the Miss New Jersey Teen title and I was full of enthusiasm, confidence and buzz from being on stage. I felt the calling to work with teens who had been bullied and could use even more confidence in their lives.

At the time, I had an after-school job at the clothing store Abercrombie & Fitch. My job mostly entailed folding shirts and spraying perfume in the air—not very connected to my love for personal development and growth. When business was slow, I would chat with my boss, Ryan. He was in his early twenties, a misplaced surfer stuck in New Jersey in a job he hated. Ryan was miserable, and being around him was such an energy drain.

One day I asked him, "Would you be open to some coaching and advice?"

He seemed surprised at first—I was just a "kid," after all. But he agreed, and I started coaching him at a little table in the back of

I had to keep practicing the lessons I was teaching.

the store. I taught him the basic principles I knew so well—what you focus on expands; stay in the present moment; gratitude is the key; and so on—and gave him assignments.

Ryan had been living a life in a state that was so far from grateful, he was hard-pressed to come up with anything he could be thankful for. I showed him that his misery was not tied to his circumstances, but to his attitude *about* his circumstances. When he understood that he would only get more of what he put out into the world, his attitude shifted. His daily gratitude practice set the *foundation* for his transformation. Because he was able to enter a state of gratefulness and thankfulness for something in his life, he left little room for focusing on the misery and opened up his world to possibilities for change. This was a *big* shift!

After only a month of working together, Ryan landed his dream job in California—at Venice Beach! His job paid three times what he made at Abercrombie, and he was able to surf every day, surround himself with like-minded people and finally make the big change he had always dreamt of. Ryan wrote an amazing testimonial about how my coaching changed his life, and that's how my business started. I was a freshman in high school, and I was already living my dream.

Gratitude is the key to happiness.

Still, as is true for everyone, I had to keep practicing the lessons I was teaching. When I faltered, or forgot to be grateful, life was much more difficult. I got my first paying client when I was seventeen. She lived in Canada. For a few weeks, I had just the one client, and that fact became my fixation point. Every day I thought, "I'm a great coach. I know a lot of people. Why don't I have more clients?"

I grew more and more frustrated, until one day I took a step back and realized I was focused on what I didn't have. Once I was aware of it, I shifted my thinking to one of gratitude, not lack. I said, "I've got this amazing client who is paying to work with me and learn from my expertise. I'm so grateful that this one person wants to work with me."

I started giving gratitude for my Canadian client every single day. Consistently, I heaped all of my love and energy onto my coaching relationship with her and gave zero focus to the fact that she was my only client. It wasn't long before I received an email with a referral for a new client; then, a week later, another referral. Two weeks after that, I received a referral for *two* new clients. I'm twenty-three now and I coach clients all over the world. It was a pinball effect; I didn't market myself. I built my business through word of mouth marketing and referrals; it was just friends telling their friends about me.

Everyone has natural gifts. Coaching is one of my many passions and gifts; I discovered it and took steps to fulfill that calling at a young age, but none of that would have been possible if I hadn't learned the principles of gratitude. It's a beautiful experience to be in gratitude and share that energy with the people I coach, the people I love and even the random people with whom I interact as I go about my day.

Make gratitude the place you return to.

Through my experience, I've found that gratitude is the key to happiness. Gratitude has the power to change your emotional state and your physical state. Those moments when you're feeling down—just as Ryan felt when I met him, and as I did when I focused on having "only one" client—being grateful is one of the most powerful ways to pull yourself out of it. There is no in between. You are either grateful, or you're not. When you make a conscious choice to be grateful and thankful, the negative feelings pass. And once you make a practice of this, those low-energy feelings will disappear so fast, you'll be amazed at your ability to shift into positivity.

Gratitude is my go-to strategy to pull myself out of a negative story, or a bad mood. Gratitude is always that rock for me, made solid and unbreakable because I practice gratitude *every single day*. Gratitude is present throughout my day, when I think of the blessings in my life and manifest my future desires. I use different strategies and tools to remind myself of this constant gratitude and blessing, which helps me to expand my own happiness, fulfillment and bliss in each moment.

Everyone I work with has their own approach to daily gratitude practice. For some it's journaling. For others it's dancing and connecting to their bodies. For my dad, it's surfing, time on the ocean to be peaceful and quiet. One of my favorite gratitude practices takes place is in my car. I choose to practice gratitude when I'm driving because it's easy to remember—I do it every time I get in my car. When I'm driving, I always give gratitude out loud, whether it's a ten-minute drive or shorter, This is time I carve out to be with my beautiful thoughts, reflect on how I'm feeling, notice what's in my heart and speak into my deepest desires for what I want to create. I use this time to manifest, tune into my higher-self and notice all the blessings that surround me in *every* moment.

When I practice gratitude, I find it is especially effective to combine thankfulness with manifestation. I express gratefulness for all that I have and enjoy in my life and would like to receive *more* of, and then I envision what I would like to attract into my life and express thanks for it in advance. I say, "I am grateful for this and I want it to continue." In this way, I keep myself in a positive, peaceful state *and* set myself up for success—all while I'm in my car! When I'm feeling grateful, I constantly attract more things to be grateful for; it is a constant circle of people, events and opportunities coming into my life.

Gratitude has up-leveled every relationship I've had in my life, especially with myself. I love myself more when I am practicing gratefulness and thankfulness. It's a life-changer. This is why I always return to gratitude. What I find so amazing and impactful is the way the people around me notice and appreciate the energy and essence that I exude, which stems from my presence to gratitude for each moment.

Make gratitude the place you return to. I recommend that you choose a gratitude ritual that seems really juicy to you and start with just five minutes of thankfulness each day. When I work with my clients, everyone starts in a different place. Some start by being grateful for their physical bodies: "I am thankful for my breath, my face, my hands." Some start with being grateful for where they are physically in that moment: "Thank you for this place, this view, this experience, this music, this room." Some want to focus on nature: "Thank you for the sun, the warmth, the breeze I feel on my body."

And some want to focus on their blessings: "I am thankful I have a job, that I have money coming in, and that I know what I *don't* want to do, so I can figure out what I *do* want."

There's no special or perfect formula. It's simple and powerful and beautiful. What are you grateful for, and what do you want to bring into your life? What would make you say each day, "I love my life"?

In my life, I've found gratitude to represent the essence of joy, peace and love. Being grateful is a "now" experience and is often a great way to bring yourself back into the present moment. I truly believe that we can all tap into something that's beautiful in our lives and give thanks for it. This takes a moment a day to change your life and it's so worth it.

Your gratitude starts *now*. Begin in this moment. Say it with me: "I love my life because…"

Chelsea Markel began her coaching practice at the age of sixteen and now works with clients all over the world, from London to Brazil. After winning the Miss New Jersey Teen title in 2008, Chelsea focused her energy and creativity on inspiring people to go after their dreams, find their voices and stand in their power. Her mission is to share simple practices that make a massive impact, so you can live a life that's even more beautiful, fulfilling and on-purpose.

Communications strategist and manager for New Peaks™, Chelsea is a copywriter known for creating powerful results for her clients who want to develop clear brand messages and market their authentic offerings to their tribes. Chelsea is also a passionate fitness instructor, certified to teach the Xtend Barre Method. Connect with Chelsea at www.ChelseaMarkel.com.

Koro Cantabrana

THERE IS ONLY PLAN A: SUCCEED

Y ou have probably heard the story about a mother lifting a car in order to free her trapped child. You've no doubt heard of mothers working several jobs to give their children the best opportunities. And it is likely you have witnessed a mother caring for an ailing child, willing her son or daughter to heal with the sheer power of her love.

Mothers are warriors. Whether you are a mother or not, there is much to learn from their example of relentless focus and determination on behalf of her children. Mothers will do whatever it takes to secure their child's health, safety and happiness. There is no back up plan, no plan B. What could you accomplish if you applied that same attitude toward your purpose in life? You wouldn't give up on a child, so why would you give up on your dream?

I experienced the power of a mother's love just moments after I gave birth to my first child, my son Alan. Labor was long and difficult. Then, when my husband was removed from the room I knew something was wrong. The medical team had to act fast.

After painful contractions and several attempts to push him out, the doctor was forced to use a tool to deliver Alan. Finally, he was here. I hugged and kissed Alan and then I rested. It seemed the big scare was over, but the worst was yet to come.

A couple of hours after he was born, I was holding Alan, feeling the love, affection and trust this precious little person placed in me. Suddenly, he began to grow cold. *Alan isn't right,* I thought. I called the nurse and she took him. Minutes later we were called to the neonatal unit. I could barely get out of bed; my body was in shock and pain after the hard delivery.

In a wheelchair, I went with my husband to the unit. Gripping my husband's hand, I waited for the doctor to give us the news. "Alan's life is endangered," the doctor said. "He has left heart hypoplasia syndrome. Only half of Alan's heart works, and it is the weakest half."

My own heart filled with sorrow. *How could this be happening?* I had waited and prepared for Alan with great joy and enthusiasm—designing his nursery; taking childbirth classes; purchasing baby clothes and supplies; dreaming of his face, his smile, his tiny hands and feet. I wanted to see him. I wanted to hug him, kiss him and take him home. I wanted to watch him grow up.

"The only option is surgery," the doctor explained. Alan was growing weaker by the minute. Without the surgery he only had

---

**"The only option is surgery," the
doctor explained.**

---

hours to live. With no available bed in any of the hospitals that performed this type of specialized operation, we found a hospital five hundred miles away and Alan was transferred immediately.

When we arrived at the new hospital, I was full of renewed hope that my son would be strong enough to face the surgery. That hope was quickly dashed when the surgeon who would be operating on Alan informed us that ninety-five percent of the children with left heart hypoplasia syndrome die on the operating table; as yet no child with this disease had ever survived the surgery in Spain.

When I was pregnant I was convinced my first son was coming into this world to be great, to do awesome things. Now there was little hope he would live to see his second day on earth. *I can't believe this is* happening, I thought, and my heart sank into utter sadness.

Then, in an instant, I knew what I had to do. I had to protect my mind from thoughts of his death.

I fixed my mind with only positive outcomes, holding fast to the illusion that everything would go well. I trusted my son, in his strength and his will to live. Though every step that day seemed a tougher test than the last, I held fast to the belief that he would be the first child with his disease to survive the complicated surgery in Spain.

Suddenly, a light illuminated the darkness. By a curious coincidence, the hospital medical team had just received specific training to operate on infants with this disease. As a means to continue to raise my hopes, I thanked everyone involved in the

---

I fixed my mind with only positive outcomes.

---

procedure: the medical team for the work they were doing to keep Alan alive; the surgeon for his expertise; the person who donated blood for transfusion. I thanked everyone for everything, and that gave my weakened energy a lift.

When they took Alan to the operating room I realized there could only be success or failure—life or death. There was no middle ground. In my heart there was only Plan A: success. And there was only one outcome: life.

After seven agonizing hours, the surgeon appeared in the waiting room. My husband and I held our breath as, again, we waited to hear news of our son. "Alan survived the operation," he exclaimed and his smile was so big it lit up his whole face.

The magic of life had won. Alan was their success story. He chose success and life! I was elated. In the dramatic hours leading up to this happy news the yearning to hug and kiss Alan had grown stronger and stronger, and soon I would be able to get my wish.

That day I was reborn. I learned how important it is to live life enjoying every breath, every smile, every touch. And yes, every thought and every emotion. At that moment I realized I had an important mission to fulfill: to be happy and to help as many people as possible achieve happiness.

I am convinced that the best way to live a successful life is to keep growing, keep dreaming, continue practicing our love and sharing our passions and to keep working for a better world. Putting this out in the world is how we attract all good things: wealth, abundance, creativity, relationships, powerful experiences and everlasting joy.

Mothers are warrior leaders and their strength can change the world.

That day I also discovered I am a warrior—a warrior mother. The author Marion C. Garrety said, "Mother love is the fuel that enables normal human beings to do the impossible." I believe that. And after my experience with Alan, I know it is absolutely true.

A great leader, like a great warrior, is bigger than any obstacle and takes action no matter what the circumstances. Warriors give thanks to the universe and all of their tribe for all they are and all they have achieved. We are now at the precise moment when we must believe in the leadership of mothers.

Mothers are warrior leaders and their strength can change the world. A great mother, like a leader, is one who helps her children feel their own power and believe in their own missions, who supports them with their visions and helps them unfold their passions and trust themselves. Whatever happens, warrior mothers will stand by their children. They will do whatever it takes to ensure positive results for them in all areas of life. They believe, without any doubt, that there will only be one outcome: success. There is only Plan A.

We need more of this kind of people in this world. And it is time to support the development and growth of mothers around the world, helping them succeed in life and find true happiness. Mothers are raising our planet's future leaders, and when a mother grows as a person, her children also grow. Her possibilities become her children's possibilities. And greater growth and possibility for children means growth and possibility for all. Supporting mothers to become bigger warrior leaders is how we change the world.

And everyone needs to support the development and growth of his or her own life, and his or her own dreams. You too. No matter your gender, no matter if you are a parent or childless, you can act as a warrior mother to your own life purpose, because we can all achieve our dreams, no matter how big they are or impossible they seem. My son Alan survived the delicate heart surgery that is the only hope for children born with his disease. They said it was impossible, but I never considered any other outcome but success. Today, Alan is a happy sixteen-year-old boy. He is homeschooled and also studies violin at a professional music school. He is here. He is wonderful. He is living a beautiful life.

Why can't you be successful achieving your goals? What does it matter if others have tried and failed? Love your dream as a mother would love her child. Tell yourself there is only one option. Leave no room for doubts, or for Plan B. For you, there is only Plan A.

Koro Cantabrana is a speaker and trainer and a certified life, business and team coach. She is founder and CEO of K7 Coaching® and IGAPPS (Inner Game Applications Spain). She guides entrepreneurs, managers and other professionals to increase their communication and leadership skills and to learn to think for success. She is known internationally for coaching elite athletes to help them reach top performance. As the founder and CEO of Mother Leader®, Koro helps moms become better leaders in the present and raise children to become better leaders in the future.

Koro earned a BA in communications from the University of Navarra, Spain; a Master's degree in photography from Santa Monica College; and a Master's degree in business administration from Foro Europeo, Spain. With a desire to see the world from the "frontlines," she started her professional career as a photojournalist. Koro worked in many different countries and showed her work at numerous exhibitions around the world, earning awards such as the 2006 "Woman in Photography International" award from Women in Photography International. Koro has taught other journalists at the prestigious University of Navarra.

In addition to articles published in books such as Sharing Bananas *by Gesmay Paynter and* Tranx Abundance *by Chema San Segundo, Koro is the co-author of the book,* Theory of Coaching. *In her work as an inspirational speaker and coach she focuses on self-empowerment, assisting people in improving their self-esteem through positive thinking. Connect with Koro at www.KoroCantabrana.com.*

Mélissa Lapierre and Nicolas Harton

You Are Already Free

It all began with a sweet little cottage. It was gorgeous and beautiful and seemed to be secluded from the world and it was just big enough for the two of us to enjoy weekends away from our home in Quebec City. But it wasn't the first cottage we loved.

We had been dreaming of a weekend place, a getaway chalet surrounded by nature, for several years, but considering our current financial picture, we thought we couldn't afford to buy a second residence. Not yet.

Shortly after we became a couple in 2006 we made a joint commitment to financial freedom. We would achieve it together; it was our life project. Our motto was: "In love, together and free!"

We knew even back then that our adventure would be a one-way trip—financial freedom or bust! We had a plan, and buying a cottage was part of that plan, but much farther down the road. We thought we had to hit specific financial milestones before we could consider purchasing a second home. Financial freedom meant being able to work when and if we pleased, and we assumed adding an additional expense would stall those plans or even move us in the wrong direction. "We're not ready," we told each other. "We will get there someday, but not today."

And yet, the conditions of the sale seemed to be an amazing opportunity, one that we needed to seize immediately. Filled with hope, we began the process that would lead to the purchase of our small corner of paradise. The meeting with the sellers was promising. The offer to purchase and the bargaining process went more smoothly than anyone would have predicted. It seemed that our long-held dream was closer than we realized!

We did hit some bumps in the road. After a few days spent working on obtaining the mortgage, the financier learned the cottage was a three-season and not fully insulated for winter and offered us a much less favorable financing plan. The new numbers

Our motto was: "In love, together and free!"

didn't add up, which made ownership of the property less and less feasible. It seemed our dream cottage was up in the sky, out of reach and coming apart, brick by brick. In the end, we were not able to purchase the cottage.

We were disappointed, but our burning desire for financial freedom was even stronger. We needed to reach it fast, now! How? Real Estate. Our plan? Acquire an income property. We then devoted all our energies to concretize this plan, sacrificing our time, our hobbies and some friends. Is that the price to pay to become free? That's what we believed.

A year and a half later, we still had not bought any income property. Nothing. Disappointed, clueless, exhausted, we asked ourselves a lot of questions. We questioned our way of doing things, our dreams, our perceptions.

Then, in 2014, we found it. The cottage was tiny—simple, charming and quiet, with a small front porch and just enough room for two. It needed some work, but with serenity all around us, the location could not be matched. We couldn't shake the feeling that it was made for us.

We said, "We have to do it." This time, the dream cottage would be ours.

Our successful purchase of our corner of paradise was the beginning of a new journey toward financial freedom. We came to understand that the path is not linear. There are ups and downs, but what's vital is making progress. It's the progress that boosts our confidence and allows us to forge ahead and take on new projects and opportunities. The process of buying our cottage sparked a realization in both of us: Even though we hadn't achieved financial freedom yet, we were already free.

Freedom is not a state of being; it's a state of mind. When we viewed purchasing our dream getaway as something we could only have if we had achieved specific milestones, we were not living free. We were not living in the present. And we were not always heeding the desires of our hearts. Purchasing the cottage, even when it seemed premature to do so, taught us that our dreams are reachable if we are simply creative in our approach.

Helping others attain financial independence was always part of our plan. At first, we thought we could only do this once we'd attained our own. But we realized the process is much more

---

We questioned our way of doing things.

---

important than the outcome. The people around us are interested in the process, and now we understand that we can help them much more than we'd initially thought. We can start right away.

By sharing our day-to-day experiences, what we've learned, and our difficulties and how we overcame them, we could give other people seeking financial freedom an opportunity to see the process up close. As we had been actively training in the field for five years and believed in the effectiveness of our training, we chose to focus primarily on real estate as a means of attaining financial independence, which prompted us to establish our own property investment company, Plan Latitude.

Knowing we are already free has allowed us to follow our hearts despite fear and doubt. We don't always know if a decision is the right one. Sometimes, we can believe that we are doing the right thing, but sometimes we doubt. This is when we make sure that our endeavors are aligned with our vision, our values and our priorities. We want all of our projects and business deals to be win-win, and to feel good for all parties.

Often we are aware that the planets are aligned for us, that we're on the right path toward financial freedom. This feeling of alignment is very rare, and we appreciate it and are grateful for it. Everything we want to occur seems to happen. We feel relaxed even if others think we "should" feel stressed. These are all signs that we are following our hearts and enjoying our freedom. When we feel that everything seems aligned, we try to integrate this state of mind deeply into our cells, so that when it occurs again, we can recognize it and be sure that we follow our hearts.

Recently we successfully flipped a property for the first time. We wanted to make money by helping people, to buy a house from someone who had a problem and needed to sell. We found one

> *Freedom is not a state of being;*
> *it's a state of mind.*

owned by a family who had inherited a house that needed a lot of work. They had started the work with the intent to sell the house, but it was too much for them.

We were creative with a very small budget, and jumped on a deal for the kitchen and bathroom before we even bought the house. We began planning the renovations. By now, we knew we had to follow our hearts and we trusted that the deal would go through. Because of our forethought, we were able to do all of the work—with the help of contractors and family—*and sold the house,* in six weeks.

In keeping with our value of win-win, the buyers also had a problem we were able to solve. They had a limited budget but needed a "turnkey house." They didn't have the time or resources to renovate any of the affordable properties. We had deliberately priced the house accessibly to attract just this kind of buyer. They were thrilled, and when the seller returned to see the house after we renovated it, she was so happy.

She said, "I'm impressed with what you did. The house has another life."

Even more than selling the house, helping people was a bigger gift.

It all began with the little cottage. We were creative in financing that property, and that gave us confidence in ourselves. We had to realize a dream to be able to realize *more* dreams. We began to see that we didn't have to wait until we achieved financial freedom to live the life we wanted or fulfill the dreams we held dear. We were free to experience all that we desired *on our path* to financial freedom.

We go to our cottage almost every weekend to get away, to take care of ourselves, to daydream, to be creative, to rest. A lot of ideas and plans came from our weekends there. And now we know we can make those ideas and plans happen right now, not down the road when, on paper, everything seems financially viable.

You don't have to be financially free to realize your dreams. You are *already* free. Determine why, deep inside, you want to attain financial freedom and make a personal commitment to yourself to do whatever it takes to succeed, but also realize that you don't have to postpone joy. Begin to think creatively, and then, when you find an opportunity to make a dream come true, follow your heart. That dream will be yours!

Mélissa Lapierre and Nicolas Harton are the founders of Plan Latitude, a creative property investment company helping homeowners and first-time buyers to attain their own financial freedom. An enthusiastic and energetic couple, they are motivated by a profound desire for freedom and seek to share their passion for commitment, personal excellence and self-fulfilment by inspiring others to strive for financial independence.

Mélissa is a communicator who writes for magazines and newspapers, sharing the stories of those who inspire her, namely entrepreneurs, real estate professionals, people with atypical career paths and committed young students. Determined to inspire, mobilize and motivate, she also hosts various events related to entrepreneurship as well as television programs focusing on such passions as travel, house and home and gardening. (www.MelissaLapierre.com.)

Nicolas, also a communicator, is a kinesiologist by trade. With his keen interest in health and education, he works with the Entrac team as a postural hygiene trainer and guest speaker, assisting hundreds of workers every year. His interventions help prevent workplace injury, which in turn enhances the productivity of businesses.

Co-founders of a theater company called the Théâtre des À-côtés, this couple made their first forays into the business world in 2007. And it didn't take long before Mélissa and Nicolas made a commitment: that of attaining financial freedom. Together.

Since embarking on their shared path, they have been learning, raising questions, progressing and evolving on a daily basis. They have turned real estate into their ticket to attaining financial independence and, to date, have participated in a wide range of training programs and seminars in Quebec and the United States. Connect with them at www.PlanLatitude.com.

Brigitte Lovell

A Strong Current

My hands gripped the wheel as I drove to the local police station with a plastic bag full of old prescription medications beside me on the passenger seat. I had been storing the pills in my house for seven months—longer, if you count the time I actually *used* them. In a few minutes, I would hand them over to the police—the only legal and safe way to dispose of prescription meds—and I would have to say goodbye to the pills forever.

Though I had been off all meds for nearly a year, I kept the half-full bottles "just in case" I needed them. Knowing the pills were in the house made me feel safe. I could access them any time; I wouldn't have to go back to the doctor and get a new prescription. The thought of letting go of the meds made me nervous, but I knew—just as I knew seven months before, that I had to stop using them: It was time.

In the summer of 2013, while visiting my grandmother and my aunt in their native Slovakia, I went to see a homeopathic doctor. It was my first visit. After his examination he said, "If you continue taking the same dosages and quantities of meds you've been on, your liver will be compromised. You need to make a change."

Before this consult, it had never occurred to me that I was hurting my body. I built a successful orofacial pain practice, and had worked hard for all I had. So what if I needed a little help getting to sleep at night? And many people are on anti-depressants—it was completely normal. Yet when the doctor told me my liver and health were at risk if I didn't stop, a light bulb went on over my head. This was serious. Was I relying too heavily on the drugs to get me through the day and night?

I thought back over the past few years. In dental school, I was on a low dose of prescription sleeping pills to help me get to and stay asleep. But during board exams, I would take three times the maximum dose every night, and sometimes keep taking that

I wanted to rely on myself, rather than on medications.

amount for months at a time. After completing dental school, my residency and a fellowship, I sought help to cope with other issues—anxiety, depression and stress. At that time, I was taking three different sleeping pills to get to sleep. My doctors added anxiolytics and anti-depressants to the mix. Over time, my medicine cabinet came to look like a mini pharmacy.

When a person is pushing hard to get through school and then working long days building a business, it's easy to fall into using prescription medications to sleep and to deal with anxiety. It makes sense, because that's what the medications are *for*. And yet, I definitely used them as a crutch. I didn't want a crutch. I wanted to rely on myself, rather than on medications.

When I returned home to the United States, I made up my mind to stop taking "these" prescription medications. There was a time when the pills served their purpose and helped me a great deal, but I knew down deep in my bones that I no longer needed them and that I could live without them without jeopardizing my health. It would be difficult to quit, but my inner voice was telling me everything would be all right.

"I don't care how I get it done, this is going to get done," I told myself. "It's time—it just is. Nothing will stop me."

Over the course of the summer, I stopped taking every single prescription medication I had been prescribed—more than four in total. I packed up the bottles and stored them out of sight, for safekeeping. Just knowing the bottles were in the house and that I could get to them quickly if I needed them made the process easier.

Going through withdrawal was challenging beyond what I anticipated. My body shifted rapidly from feeling hot to so cold I got the shivers. My muscles ached. I was dizzy and nauseous and perspiring even inside air-conditioned spaces. My hands shook so much I had to hide them so no one would notice. I felt as though I had a dark cloud looming over me at all times.

That summer, I did nothing but work and go home. I could function at my practice, but outside of work I felt miserable physically, emotionally and mentally from the withdrawal. I walked through my time away from work in a daze, foggy and disoriented. I couldn't concentrate. Because of this I had a hard

I felt as though I had a dark cloud looming over me at all times.

time talking with people, or being around friends, so I isolated. Other than engaging in professional conversations, I rarely spoke with anyone. *No one will understand what I'm going through,* I thought. *I can't even understand what I'm going through!*

The withdrawal symptoms made me more distant and aloof. I was absent from important gatherings. I felt like an emotional alien, just trying to seem normal when I was anything *but* normal. Even after I was completely off the medications, I continued to have the withdrawal symptoms for a couple of months, until the meds were flushed out of my body.

The symptoms were so intense, I started to wonder if life was worth living, which is a common side effect from stopping the medications I had been taking. The only thing that kept me going was my inner voice, that strong current of certainty that helped me make the decision to stop using the pills and carried me through months of hell. I kept telling myself, *Somehow, some way, the symptoms will end and you will feel better.*

As the withdrawal subsided, I *did* start to feel better. I also began to think clearly. Because of the medications, I had felt numb for many years. In my new state, I experienced emotions that had

---

Off of the meds, I began to see with a different set of eyes.

---

been dormant for quite some time. As the glass barrier between my true heart and my true feelings lifted, my inner voice grew stronger and louder. I became a warmer person, a happier person, a more *authentic* person. True to myself for perhaps the first time in my life, I felt like a newly hatched chick experiencing the world. Off of the meds, I began to see with a different set of eyes.

And yet always in the back of my mind, I knew my stash of pills was available to me. I thought about the summer of withdrawal, how I made up my mind and that, despite the agony I went through, and the helplessness I felt, I never gave up. *I trusted myself.* And I could trust myself again.

Walking into the police station, my "security blanket" clutched to my chest, I knew I would be okay. Just as I was certain I could wean myself off the meds, I knew I could say goodbye to them for good. It was a defining moment for me, handing over the plastic bag of pill bottles I hadn't opened in months. And in that moment I realized: *I am the solution. The solution lies within me, not in external tools, not in other people's ideas or promises. I will never turn back.*

I've been off prescription medications for two years now. I'm still re-learning how to be in the world, and re-experiencing myself. I can sleep without medications. Though I still have transient and minimal anxiety, I think clearly and I can manage without medications. I am in control of my life and my emotions—without medications. I have a greater sense of awareness of my being. I am far more powerful than I ever dreamed possible and I am excited about living and the possibilities life has to offer.

Within all of us is a strong current, a determination that can see us through any challenge and help us reach any goal. This current was in me all along, I just needed to tap into it; I just needed to know it was there and let it carry me through to achieve my goal.

This current is within you, too. No matter what you struggle with, you can choose healthier behaviors that will help you transform your life. There is no pill, no system, no program, no book and no person who can do it for you. *You are the solution.* Listen to your heart, that inner voice inside of you that tells you when the time is right to take action, and then go for it! Make up your mind and then promise yourself: I will never turn back.

Disclaimer: I am not recommending that everyone come off their medications. There are individuals who must have these medications to function and live life. This message is only for individuals who do not have severe life-threatening conditions. Only you and your health care professional can decide if my method is right for you.

Brigitte Lovell is the Director for the Keeler Center for Headache & Orofacial Pain. She is a dentist who treats and manages acute and chronic pain patients to include management of all aspects of chronic refractory headache disorders such as migraine, tension–type headache, cluster headache, post-traumatic headache and occipital neuralgia. In addition, she treats patients with orofacial pain conditions encompassing musculoskeletal pain (TMJ/TMD), neurovascular and neuropathic pain.

Dr. Lovell also has significant training in dental sleep medicine and fabricates dental sleep appliances for obstructive sleep apnea and snoring. Her headache and orofacial pain training result from completing a neurology headache fellowship at the Jefferson Headache Center in Philadelphia under Dr. Stephen Silberstein preceded by completion of residency training in orofacial pain at the University of California, Los Angeles (UCLA). She is a graduate of the inaugural dental class of the Arizona School of Dentistry and Oral Health. Dr. Lovell attended the University of Texas at Austin for undergrad and majored in the Czech language.

Growing up in El Paso, Texas, Brigitte began playing the piano at age four and participated in many piano recitals and competitions, earning the Paderewski medal, among other honors. She has visited many countries in Europe. Her grandmother and aunt live in Slovakia where she spent the majority of her summers. She is fluent in both the Slovak and Czech languages. Connect with Dr. Brigitte Lovell at www. KeelerCenterForPain.org.

Fernand Pors

Living with Purpose

No matter where you are on the personal development path—whether you're just starting out or have already many walked many miles—you probably know that finding your true purpose is a key component to living a successful, fulfilling, joyful life, however you define it. But what if you haven't found your purpose? What if you've searched and searched and still don't know what you are called to do? What if no matter how much you've read, experienced and explored, you still don't know what makes you feel alive?

I believe that we are here on this planet to enjoy life fully and have amazing experiences, and to live in accordance with who we are, with our inner truths and values, and to use our talents to make a positive contribution. Yet for many years, I was unable to figure out what made *me* feel alive and to what I wanted to devote my life.

After I finished my study of electrical engineering, I was very motivated to work in my field. However, after a few years I found myself in a job that didn't fulfill me. The work didn't excite me anymore. I was deeply bored, uninspired in the dull familiarity of my daily routines and couldn't see anything exciting in my future. My work as an electrical engineer didn't give me the meaningful experiences I was longing for; my heart wasn't in the work. *Life is passing me by,* I thought. *I'm wasting my time, my talents and ultimately my life. This isn't how I want to live.*

I had no idea how to get out of the situation because I had no idea how or where to *find* fulfillment. I tried to find solutions in personal growth books and from experts on the Internet, and I took some personal development trainings, but did not find a solution that really helped me find the answers that I was looking for. When I realized all the research I had done had not yielded anything substantial, I felt frustrated and hopeless, as if my life was out of my control. *I'm trapped and I can't find a way out.*

Then I entrusted a lady I met at a workshop discussing with her my struggle. "I've searched everywhere I can think of," I said. "And nothing I found has led to anything that inspires me."

Her reply helped me to make a big realization. She said, "This theme of finding your purpose plays such a role in your life. Could it be the clue to your purpose?"

I had never looked at it like that before. I knew there was a deep truth in what she said. At first I was too overwhelmed to respond. Then I gradually started to realize that the source of years of

Most people haven't become aware of what their purpose is.

frustration could actually be the clue to my purpose. Rather than fight against my perceived "lack of purpose," what if I looked at it from a different perspective? *What if the search is the point?* What if my purpose was helping other people find meaning in their lives?

That was the realization that changed my life. A new life began for me that day; I felt liberated and full of inspiration. I had the energy and enthusiasm I remembered having when I was a child. I was so relieved, so full of joy. Something fundamental in my life had finally fallen into place.

All of that frustration, all of my searching—it turned out to be a blessing in disguise. Since that moment, I have continued my research and training and I began building a business to help people find and live their life purposes. At the moment of writing this, I still work part time at my engineering job, and spend a good part of the remaining time on my new "vocation". My activities seem much different now as I have a vision of where I am going. Some activities that used to annoy me before I became aware of my purpose took on new meaning because I can make them fit in a bigger plan.

As energizing it can be to have an inspiring purpose to "pursue," it's important to be aware that joy is not achieved just by finding something inspiring and meaningful to strive for in the future, but also by the awareness of being blessed in the present moment, independent of your circumstances. There is joy in the here and now.

Be aware of all the things you can
already be grateful for in your life.

You can experience "purpose moments" every day. Actually, that's the point of living with purpose. In his book, *Life's Golden Ticket*, Brendon Burchard shares three questions we will ask ourselves at the end of our lives:

- Did I live? (Fully, vibrantly, passionately?)
- Did I love? (Openly, honestly, with all my heart?)
- Did I matter? (Did I make a difference? Was there a purpose for me? How did I contribute?)

Now is the moment to consider these questions, as there is time to live more in alignment with the answers to these questions that appeal to you; don't wait until it's too late. If you look for them, every day has opportunities to live, love and matter—*here and now*.

We live in a world that is changing faster than ever. Our world is full of distractions with new technologies, social media, entertainment, commitments and so on. It's easy to be busy all day, forgetting to take the time to consider whether all of our activities lead to something worthwhile. This causes many people to feel stressed, frustrated and unfulfilled.

Further, big traditional institutions in religion, government, health care and finance, for example, have been alienating themselves more and more from society. The certainties that many people believed they could rely on are eroding more and more. I believe that this process will continue and will cause many who rely on these institutions to be disillusioned in the coming years.

This is why discovering your purpose in life and living it is more important than ever. It allows you to cut through all of the noise and focus on what really matters to you.

There are many "benefits" of living with purpose. These are three of them:

Living with Purpose Gives You Confidence, Inspiration and Energy

As your purpose is part of the essence of who you are, it gives you an inner drive, inspiration and energy. You have something you believe in and won't let obstacles or difficulties stop you easily. Opinions of other people affect you less, because you are more determined. You have more willingness to step out of your comfort zone. That's what gives you more personal power and you achieve more as a consequence.

Living with Purpose Focuses Your Energy in One Direction

When you know what your purpose is, you know where to direct your energy and attention. It also makes it easier to decide which potential activities you can refrain from, by seeing whether or not they are in alignment with your purpose. Many small steps *in one direction* lead to progress in the long term. You are going somewhere! You can compare it to a magnifying glass. When you hold it in the sun and you focus it on one point, it has the power to burn a hole in a piece of wood. But when you focus it at many different spots, there isn't much power and nothing will happen.

Living with Purpose Makes You Feel Alive and Fulfilled

When you live on purpose, you know that what you're doing resonates with the essence of who you are and why you're here.

That gives deeper meaning to your life and inner peace. You're expressing a deep dimension in yourself that's authentic, which makes you feel alive and happy.

In addition to these three "personal benefits," living in alignment with your purpose usually means that you'll have a positive impact in the world, as your purpose transcends your personal interests. That's what the world needs now, as we see too many examples of unfortunate consequences of people who have pursued their personal benefits regardless of the negative impact of their actions, such as damaging or polluting nature, ill-treating animals, exploiting people, corruption, abuse of power and so on. We need many more people living a purposeful life in order to create a peaceful, just and sustainable world that we can pass on to the next generations.

Many people ask themselves: "What do I love to do?" Although it's a great question to ask yourself, purpose is about expressing a deep dimension in yourself from an inner wisdom of why you're here. Thought leader and author of *The Power of Now,* Eckart Tolle said, "Instead of asking, 'What do I want from life?' a more powerful question is 'What does life want from me?'"

I believe everybody has an individual purpose, but that most people haven't become aware of what their purpose is. Your purpose is a part of the essence of who you are. The place to discover your purpose is in yourself. Other people may help you to discover it, but you are the only one who has the inner knowledge of what's true for you.

Here are five areas to explore to get more clarity about your purpose:

1. Explore your strong feelings. What makes you feel alive, and excited, what moves you deeply, which activities allow you to express the essence of who you are? Looking at your answers, specifically what about these activities gives you such a great feeling?

2. Explore your biggest frustrations, from right now or in the past. Have you experienced a situation or incident that was painful and had a big emotional impact on you? Instead of focusing on the painful side of such experiences, realize that they may turn out to be a blessing to you if you look at them from a different perspective. What have you learned from it and how has learning that improved your life? How could you help people who experience a similar situation to overcome their challenge?

3. Explore your gifts and talents. Which gifts and talents do you use at your "most shining moments"? What special gifts and talents come to you naturally? And how can you use them to make a valuable contribution for other people, or (using Eckart Tolle's words) use them "as life wants from you"?

4. Explore your essence. Imagine you're old and at the end of your life. How would you like to look back at your life? What kind of person would you want to have been? What has your life been about? What impact did you have on other people? Is there something you would like to leave behind as a legacy or gift?

5. Explore your desire for contribution. Which causes do you deeply care about and strongly believe in? What does the world or do people need more of?

Note: For practical reasons I have mentioned ways that I can give to you in a book; there are other ways to find clues to your purpose such as a guided meditation, that I provide in workshops, as it's more suitable to do that in live sessions.

Finally, looking at your answers and insights from these five areas, take those that most strongly resonate with you, and combine them in two or three sentences that include the *three Es of Purpose*:

- *Your Essence,* who you are when you live in alignment with your purpose

- *Your Expression,* the talents and activities through which you love to express yourself, and

- The *Effect* or impact that your purpose inspires you to create in your environment or in the world

For example: "I am a loving, enthusiastic and playful person. I organize and build connections to create a community where people blossom and support each other."

Finding your purpose is not a one-time activity. When you come back to it regularly, you'll clarify and refine your purpose more and more over time. Living on purpose is not just about achieving things in the "outside" world, it's also about finding joy in the moment. And that's what you can find inside, independent of your outside circumstances. Don't make your happiness dependent on something that doesn't exist yet. If you do that, you will never feel fulfilled.

You can find joy in the present moment, even for no reason at all. Living with purpose is not just about achieving things in the "outside" world, it's also about finding joy in the moment. See the beauty in yourself and the world around you. Be aware of all the things you can already be grateful for in your life.

If you don't find your purpose right away, it doesn't mean you don't have one. People who have gone through a similar experience and found answers can be of great help to you. It's in your heart and soul where you'll find your purpose and who you want to be in this world.

After years of feeling uninspired and frustrated as he struggled to find his true purpose, Fernand Pors discovered a process for shifting his perspective and created a life he loves. Now he supports others to do the same. An engineer by trade, Fernand has extensive training in personal development. As a transformational coach, he combines his technical knowledge and spiritual focus to provide a practical, no-nonsense method of helping people to connect with who they are, and who they want to be—without having to spend years of painstaking and unproductive effort to find solutions on their own.

Fernand gives workshops in the Netherlands and offers international clients online education opportunities, such as his 7-Step Process to Clarify Your Purpose video series and his 1-hour Ignite Your Life teleseminar. Connect with Fernand at www.YourPurpose.life.

Brittany Rachelle

CALM BEFORE THE STORM

A storm was building in my mind. A plethora of negative emotions whirled in my brain—anger, disappointment, helplessness. I couldn't turn off the constant string of negative thoughts: *I'm worthless. I don't matter. I'm not a good kid. If they only knew my secret...*

My cheeks grew warm and my breath quickened. I was in a panic, blinded by my thoughts and feelings I couldn't control. My mind was running wild with all of the things I did or said wrong that day, that week: *I will never be perfect. I'm not the perfect daughter, the perfect friend, the perfect weight, the perfect student, the perfect sister, the perfect girlfriend, the perfect athlete.*

Suddenly, I collapsed onto the floor. I was inconsolable, crying alone in my room, so disappointed I couldn't hold in my emotions. "Why am I so weak? Why can't I handle things like normal people," I said out loud.

I thought, *if I don't act immediately, I will never be able to calm down. I'll never be able to fully release my pain.* I knew what I had to do. I had been doing it for years. I had to cut.

At age eleven, I inherited feelings of low self-esteem and low self-worth. I became inactive and unhappy and I felt lost. I buried myself in my room with books and music, thinking, *being alone isn't as lonely if it's my choice.*

In seventh grade I was introduced to an unorthodox means of self-destruction in the form of self-injury, specifically cutting. After I would cut, a calm would settle in, a calm I never felt otherwise. My eyes would gradually close, my breathing would steady and my mind would finally be at peace. There were no more arguments going on in my head about whether or not I should just act and relax; next time I would be strong enough to stop the panic and pain without cutting.

I can't explain the incredible release of anything bad or negative straining my mind after I inflicted my own pain or the amount of

*I knew what I had to do. I had been
doing it for years. I had to cut.*

control I felt over my body and my senses. My action put me at ease. This feeling of being untouchable was addicting. I felt invincible.

If I couldn't sleep, the solution was to cut. If I didn't do my homework, the solution was to cut. If I said the wrong thing, the solution was to cut. I knew that high after the act would never last forever, but there was always next time. I told myself, "One day I will be able to overcome that urge." One day the part of my brain that knew all along that self-injury was not the answer to everything would win the war, but in the meantime, I would enjoy my calm before the next storm.

To protect my ability to "self-heal" in the manner I saw fit, I knew I couldn't let anyone in. If no one knew about my dark secret, no one would pity me, or try to watch out for me and make me stop. I wanted to be able to continue using cutting as a means to calm my mind and body as long as *I* needed it and to quit only when *I* decided it was time. I only let a select few into my secret life, friends who also used self-injury to "self-heal."

The fear of being caught terrified me. That fear also kept me from allowing the secret to be read on my face. To everyone who didn't know the real me, I was an extrovert, I was happy. I knew that in order to keep my secret, I had to continue to be perceived as "normal." I had to be involved in sports, I had to have friends and I had to do well in school. I also knew I would one day grow out of my self-destructive phase, which is the only reason I never completely ruined everything else in my life. I thought, *I need every other aspect of my life to work out, so that when I grow out of this problem, I'll have a safety net.*

If I could curb my bad habits and learn to handle difficult emotions and situations in a healthy manner, and if I could begin to hang out with a different crowd of people who also knew how to manage their emotions in a healthy way, I would have a lot going for me.

The longer I went without people knowing my dark secret, the more untouchable I felt. Then one night, I had a complete breakdown. Nothing in particular set me off, but I soon found myself drinking and crying so hard that breathing was a challenge. I wanted to scream, to rip up all of the pictures and posters on my

I was becoming someone I couldn't control anymore.

wall, to write letters to my friends and family and then sit in a corner and self-injure until the calm returned. I thought, *I just need to calm myself down before I do anything drastic and need to ask for help.*

This time, my "self-healing" was different. I didn't care about being discreet with my cuts; I was more concerned with calming myself down. As a result, I ended up injuring my entire left arm, from top to bottom. Never had I been that reckless or bold.

After the episode, I looked at the wreckage I had caused in my room. I looked down at my arm, and became frightened of *myself.* I was becoming someone I couldn't control anymore. My self-injuring was more than a way to sleep and calm my emotions; it was becoming a monster, one that I was not prepared to battle. I thought, *If I let the monster run free, it will lead me down a dark path.*

I thought about my two little sisters. With all of my focus on myself, I hadn't been the best sister to them. Now, I was about to let out a monster that would be visible to the world. I didn't want to set a bad example for them.

That night, I decided my behavior had to change. I wanted to be a good influence. I wanted to overcome my urge to self-injure so I could one day help others through the same situations. I spent years analyzing myself, focusing on self-improvement by trying to identify *what* was causing the feelings and emotions that were

---

I was the cause of all my negative feelings,
thoughts, actions and reactions.

---

driving me to my dark habit. Once I had determined the cause, I was able to gain better understanding as to *why* I was so drawn to this type of "feelings management."

As I began to understand the reason, I was finally able to begin countering the part of my mind that wanted to resort to self-injury to "solve all my problems" and try to build new habits. I realized that I was the cause of all my negative feelings, thoughts, actions and reactions. Everyone else I knew was happy and didn't suffer from my same addiction, so why should I make myself suffer?

My self-injuring continued on and off for another four years—only in extreme situations, and only when it was convenient and I could cover the evidence. During this time, the need to self-injure slowly diminished until I realized that I would never be able to close that chapter of my life completely without asking for help. My dark habit had some closure my senior year in college when, with the help of my best friend, I finally got the courage to attend therapy.

I have been self-injury free for over a year now and for the first time, that method of "feelings management" is not my first or second thought. This is the first time I have managed to withstand my "urge" for an entire year. I graduated from college with a degree in engineering management and was hired by a company I had interned with the previous summer. Handling my problems in a healthy and constructive manner, I have never felt so content.

Author Carl Frederick said, "Life is a game, a game with no ethic until you acknowledge the truth: you are the source of it all. You and you alone are responsible for your life and the cause of all your experiences. The sole purpose of life is to acknowledge that, then choose to be what you know you are… knowing where you're going is all you need to get there." I believe that. In the simplest terms, Frederick is saying, "life is what you make of it." It's important to acknowledge, however, that nothing is permanent. Sometimes we make bad decisions or form bad habits, but that doesn't mean that those decisions or habits define who we are.

When you categorize yourself, or let other categorize you, as troubled, or difficult or a failure, your life becomes a self-fulfilling prophecy. Take responsibility for your thoughts and actions, yes, but don't fixate on the mistakes you've made or the unhealthy coping mechanisms you've used to get through the day. Self-discovery is a journey. It doesn't matter how you get there, just that you understand the necessity of making change and begin to act upon it.

The importance of self-discovery lies in the understanding of how you think, how you feel and most importantly, why. If you can determine the reason why you think, feel and act in unhealthy ways, you're in great shape to begin making the changes you need to improve your life. I have spent the last eleven years trying to understand the reasoning behind all my actions and reactions. Even though I am in a better place, I still keep myself in check and manage my urges, but the journey has become simple. I wake up every day happy with the life I have created for myself regardless of what happened yesterday. Life is such a fragile thing, and it's a shame to waste any part of it hurting oneself.

Brittany Rachelle is an industrial engineer in South Florida and an aspiring author currently working on an inspirational book for teens based on her experiences with self-injury. She received her BS in engineering management and industrial engineering from the University of Arizona in 2013. She is an active traveler, enjoys trying new things and spending time with her boyfriend, friends and family. Connect with Brittany at www.BrittanyRachelle.com.

Miriam Muñoz

Make the Best of Each Day

When I was a little girl, my favorite days were weekends because I didn't have to be awakened by an alarm clock. The way I would wake up was always the same: My mother would be the first one up in the morning; she would turn on the stereo and start singing and dancing around the house while doing chores. I would always wake up to music.

Sometimes I would remember my dreams, and somehow the music was also part of those dreams. Those memories of waking up to a happy mom and sharing weekend mornings with the whole family have stayed with me forever.

As I grew older my mornings were not so lovely. For whatever reason, I would stay up late, or sleep with the television on, or have a big meal in the evening, always garnering the same result: not enough rest at night and starting every day dragging myself out of bed, late and exhausted, wishing I could stay in bed.

I couldn't think clearly and found it difficult to make decisions or remember what I had done that day. It was as if I was always tired and half asleep, dreading my life. Because I wasn't able to pay attention, I signed over to his wife the house I had bought with my father, for which I made payments, and did not get a penny for it. I ignored my colleagues' advice to sell my stock in Lucent

Technologies—the bulk of my 401K—and ended up losing one hundred percent of my savings in the crash of the early 2000s.

When I started exploring myself and learning different empowering techniques, I was in a very low place. I had material success, but I wasn't happy. I grew up thinking, *I will get my degrees, get a good job and then live happily ever after.* I had a good education, which allowed me to succeed in the world, but I wasn't satisfied. Something was missing.

At an emotional release program with Debbie Ford at the Chopra Center I began to realize that I am not my material achievement, that I am body, mind and spirit and that all of those parts need to be nourished. Debbie talks about gratitude and about saying

---

It was as if I was always tired and half asleep.

"Thank you for this beautiful day" every day when you wake up. Or, if you are tired, saying, "Thank you for getting up." I started practicing saying, "Thank you for getting up" every morning. It became almost mechanical. Some days I didn't believe it, but I kept at it.

One day, I felt it—I felt the deep appreciation for this gift of life we have all been given. Something shifted inside of me. I thought, *This moment, and each day, is a gift, and we need to be grateful and appreciative and make the best we can of this day, of today.*

Once I came to see and understand this, it made all the difference. I discovered how important it is to take care of my body. I remembered how I used to wake up on weekend mornings and how that beautiful start set the stage for a wonderful day. I started noticing how my evening habits were making an impact on my rest. I had no idea how harmful sleeping with the television on was for my health. I had done this for decades, not realizing it impeded sleep and studies show it could cause depression.

These days, I make sure to I turn the television off and do something empowering right before I go to bed. I have nightly rituals that end with saying a little prayer or doing a relaxation exercise, focusing on one body part at a time. When I have a big problem or a question to solve, I usually make sure I think about it before going to sleep. The next day I either have the answer or know the next step to take.

Shifting from harmful habits to taking care of myself at night enabled me to wake up restored and in a positive mood. Now, every morning I am peaceful, happy and looking forward to making the best of each day. As part of my new self-care rituals, I make sure I have a relaxed time before going to bed, make sure my evening meal is lighter and I have enough time between eating and going to bed, but the most impactful habit I have built is controlling the first thought I have when I wake up.

The first thing you think of when you wake up is very important and sets the stage for your day. Adam Markel, CEO of New Peaks (formerly Peak Potentials) recommends waking each day with this thought: "I love my life." I met a woman at a New Peaks event who had created a habit of waking her kids each day by asking them,

> *The first thing you think of when*
> *you wake up is very important.*

"How are you doing?" She taught each of her children to answer, "I love my life." Imagine the kind of life these children will lead because they have started building this habit so young. I can't wait to see where they will end up. What a wonderful gift their mother has given them!

I have adopted other morning rituals as well. After I greet the day with a statement of intent and gratitude, I sit in silence and quiet my mind to achieve clarity. I used to watch the news when I was getting ready for work. Now I have a podcast or an audio book or music on in the background while I get ready. I choose what to listen to, rather than letting the television or radio decide what I need to hear. That way I always start my day in a positive mood.

John Kehoe suggests a different morning affirmation/gratitude statement, which I often use: "Miracles shall follow miracles.

Wonders shall never cease. I give thanks for this perfect day." And Anthony Robbins talks about having music that inspires us. He suggests we get up, turn it on and jump around for a bit to get our blood flowing. I do this, too.

I find that all of these techniques work effectively and help me to make every day my best day.

I recorded my voice on my iPhone and I use that as my alarm clock, instead of the radio or an obnoxious beeping sound. I have several recordings of my favorite inspirational songs, and my voice and the songs serve as alarms throughout the morning as I get ready for my day.

Having the right habits improves the quality of my life. These are simple rituals; they don't require much effort or time. It's just a matter of making them part of your routine, like brushing your

---

Practice being in the moment now.

---

teeth. Life is made up of simple steps. Brushing your teeth is simple, and yet it is very a very powerful tool in preventing tooth decay.

Rather than beat yourself down and engage in negative thinking, talk to yourself kindly and lovingly. Just try it—stick with it for a week. At first it may seem fake. You might hear your mind saying, "Sure, like it's that simple to have a good day and feel better about yourself." Just keep doing it. You will notice a difference. As the saying goes, the journey of one thousand miles begins with a single step.

Now that I have practiced better nighttime and morning rituals, I find that not only are my mornings wonderful, but I am able to cut through the noise of the world—and my own thoughts—and hear the quiet voice within, guiding my steps. The heart whispers to us softly, very softly. In order for us to hear, we need to quiet the noise. Getting in touch with nature is one way to hear your heart's whisper. Take a silent walk outside, preferably barefoot so your feet touch the grass.

Practice being in the moment now. Eckhart Tolle talks about the "just one minute now" practice. Start a habit of taking one minute when you get in your car to look around. Say, "I am here now, in this moment. I notice my hands. I look at the colors that surround me. I smell the different scents in the environment. I am just stopping and for a moment being present."

When you pay attention to the now, you can listen and hear your heart. Set the stage for your very best day. Start with simple rituals you can implement for no cost and for little time and effort. Within days you will notice a marked difference. You will feel better, more energized and more aware. Soon, you will incorporate more helpful rituals into your life, rituals you discover on your own. Let your heart guide you in choosing these rituals.

You will know you've chosen the right habits and practices based on how effortless they seem. You will begin to feel as though you are swimming with the current, rather than against it. Everything will get easier, and you will start to find joy in the simplest things. As Joseph Campbell said, "… Doors would open where there wouldn't be doors for anyone else… and there is something about the integrity of life that the world moves in and helps."

Begin today. What will you tell yourself as you go to sleep? What will you give thanks for in the morning?

Miriam Muñoz is passionate about working with individuals who seek clarity, healing or wish to begin or continue on their path to personal growth and empowerment. She believes we were all born with unique, special gifts and are divinely meant to live with passion, love, joy and abundance. Her mission is to step toward more self-knowledge and understanding of how this perfect mind/body system can be used to have an even better quality of life, systemize that knowledge and share it.

Miriam would like to make the task of the next generation easier by condensing her knowledge so that it can be absorbed in simple, easy-to-follow steps that, once integrated into regular routines, will improve the quality of people's lives.

As part of her extensive training, she has learned from Deepak Chopra, Anthony Robbins, Wayne Dyer, Sivananda, Paramahansa Yogananda, John Kehoe, Adam Markel, Debbie Ford and Brendon Burchard, just to name a few. Miriam has a Master's degree in computer science, an MBA in global business management and a Master's degree in project management. For twenty-five years she has been working as a software developer and project manager with major companies such a Bell Laboratories, NASA, Motorola, Google and Panasonic Avionics. Connect with Miriam at www.Facebook.com/MiriamMunozmp.

Julia Erickson

PERFECT TIMING

At the top of the hill, I waited. And waited. And waited. No one came.

At a weeklong leadership retreat, the facilitators had broken us into teams and tasked us with completing a course that I knew would be too demanding for me. But not wanting to hold them back or receive what I perceived to be special treatment, I had kept my physical limitations hidden from my team.

I was the designated leader. I gave instructions to the team and as I trekked to the top of the hill, I assumed everyone was behind me. When I reached the top and discovered I was alone and no one was following me, I burst into tears. After more than twelve years running nationally recognized nonprofits, I thought I knew what it meant to be a leader. How had I gotten so out of sync with my team? Exhausted and in pain after pushing myself beyond my physical ability, I felt like a failure.

Eventually, one of the facilitators came to find me. We talked about being honest with my team and relying on them to help me and about me achieving *my* one hundred percent and helping them in the ways I can. This experience led me to realize that I have a lot to offer and that my work is to find a way to offer it within my capacity and in a way that others can use it. There always will be a way.

What happened on the hill that day was a breakdown and then a breakthrough that enabled me to start looking at my heart as the yardstick instead of what other people thought of me. Rather than feed my ego and concern myself with how I appeared in the world, I asked myself, "What's *my* one hundred percent? Where does *my* heart lead me? What's *my* gut telling me?" That week was a turning point for me. I had felt successful for a long time under old circumstances. Now I needed to adapt to new circumstances and appreciate my new abilities. I had to learn new things, gain new skills, write a new script.

In the span of just a few years I had relocated from Manhattan to New Jersey; had hip replacement that left me in a lot of pain; contracted Lyme disease, which required me to have three spine surgeries and recurring back pain; gained fifty pounds as a result of all of my health issues; and had to abandon my twenty-five

I wanted to use my own experiences and accomplishments to benefit others.

year career working with nonprofits because I could no longer consistently work full time or commute to New York City. More devastating than all of that change was the loss of my six-year-old nephew—with whom I was very close—to cancer after a two-year struggle. It was time to start anew.

I began to adapt to my changed circumstances: "big brain, little body." I asked myself, "What is my new path?" I needed to find work I could do from home using technology, while still doing what I loved best and what I *knew* best: helping people. My new work had to be varied, intellectually stimulating and challenging. I wanted to use my own experiences and accomplishments to benefit others. And whatever I did, I had to have enough time to write.

In my work at City Harvest and other nonprofits, I had used the "coach approach" to management, helping staff and colleagues develop their skills and get promotions. My work with my own coach of twelve years had helped me to take City Harvest from near obscurity to being "one of New York City's best-loved charities," according to *The New York Times*. Could I be a coach? That path certainly fit all my criteria.

With a new aim in mind, I focused not on reaching the heights I once achieved as an executive director in the nonprofit sector, but on putting one foot in front of the other. I got a Master's in

---

Between the "before" and "after"
pictures is a whole lot of resistance,
reckoning and revelation.

---

business administration online. I offered free coaching, and from my first client eventually received so many referrals I've never had to market my services. Building on my expertise and experience, I started to develop a coaching system for people to find their "right fit" work. Then, I built up a social media presence around that subject.

I've spent the last eight years helping people find and secure work they absolutely love to do, work that fulfills them, work that speaks to their hearts and aligns with their life missions.

Recently I attended my thirty-fifth reunion at Smith College. The theme of the weekend was transition. In conversation after conversation, my friends and peers talked about confronting major life changes. It seemed everyone was in that mode, talking about divorce, or kids moving out, or dealing with aging parents. Many people were looking for a new job or career, having either been fired or discovered that their work was no longer fulfilling for them.

As I listened to the conversations, I was reminded of my own journey. Facing the reality of losing my purpose—my identity— was a frustrating and confusing process. In the letting go and the looking forward is an obstacle course of emotions that can derail even the most positive person. Big life changes rarely happen as they do in the movies. Rather than one climactic moment that brings about a radical change in circumstances, there is typically a sequence of events that forces us to shift our goals and priorities. Between the "before" and "after" pictures is a whole lot of resistance, reckoning and revelation.

One of the things I needed to learn to do, and what many of my clients have learned to do, is to actually *feel the feelings* that are going on instead of shutting them off. If I was very sad or angry or disappointed or exasperated—any of those so-called negative feelings—the voice in my head would say, "You shouldn't feel this

---

**You'll get to the top of the hill
when you get there.**

---

way. You can't feel sorry for yourself." I started treating myself as if I were my best friend. Or as if I were the idealized parent some of us have, the one who says, "You know, honey, you get to feel sorry for yourself for a little while." Anytime I heard the word *should* in my brain, I learned to stop and say to myself, "There's nothing you should do. Just be where you are right now."

My transition was really personal strategic planning. Strategic planning exercises begin with a current situation assessment, which means looking at the good, the bad and the ugly—the strengths, weaknesses, opportunities and threats. *Feelings are a big part of my current situation. If I start this process by feeling all of my feelings, then I can get to a place of acceptance. From there, I can take action.* So the first objective in my transition process was to be really kind to myself. I became willing to go to any lengths to feel good about myself. Now, any time I hear myself think, *oh, you're an idiot*, I say, "Honey, you are not an idiot. You are doing the best you can. Just start again." I cultivated a compassionate heart toward myself and others.

During periods of transformation, especially after a loss, well-meaning people will give advice. It's as if they can't help themselves. They mean it to be encouraging, but all of their good intentions can become overwhelming. I gave myself permission to do only what was in front of me, to do what I was motivated to do. I kept telling myself, "If that is the right thing to do, you'll get to it." I learned to be generous in my response to people's advice, but I stopped thinking I had to take action on every suggestion they made.

I discovered there is no such thing as procrastination. It is a beat-yourself-up word, and I won't beat myself up. I know that if I'm not doing something there are a number of reasons. Maybe I said "yes" to something I didn't want to do simply because I felt I should. Or, I may not have enough information to complete the task. And it's possible the reason could be that I'm afraid—afraid of failure, or putting myself out there or of making mistakes.

Transitioning from one identity to the next brings up a lot of fear. I learned a long time ago the cure for almost any fear is to imagine the worst that could possibly happen. Generally, the feared outcome is totally ridiculous. For me, it always ended with me as a bag lady in Grand Central Station. I developed an acronym for fear that helps me remember the ridiculous nature of my anxiety: Faithless Ego Anticipates Ruin. When I look at the absurd outcome I can laugh and say, "It's not going to be *that* bad." Then, I can calm down and, in the spirit of being kind to myself, say, "You're not going to be perfect, but you'll do what you can do given all of your constraints."

That day on the hill at leadership camp, I realized I needed to be a different kind of leader——less a doer and more a facilitator and supporter. That week, I transformed almost immediately into a leader who was praised for bringing the team together. In a group project later that week, I focused on encouraging people to do their best, finding out what help they needed and getting other team members to provide that help and keeping all of us focused on why we were doing the exercise. I was part of the team, not ahead of it.

In redefining leadership for myself I was able to consider coaching as a career. Today I encourage others to find the leader in themselves. I help them develop confidence in their abilities and give them the information and tools they need to market themselves effectively. Now, rather than wait for my clients to catch up, I walk with them every step of the way. I am the guide, and we travel the path together—we find out what they really want to do for work, and then get them as close to as possible given their circumstances. We identify the "top" of their hill and gradually move toward it.

When your purpose shifts—when you've lost your job, or the kids don't need you anymore, or your marriage breaks up or the parents you've been caring for die—it is difficult to cope with your new identity. What do people want from you now? What do you want from yourself? *For* yourself? What if it's too late for you to transition successfully? What if you're too old, or your health is too poor, or you aren't educated enough or don't have enough experience?

Be kind to yourself. All timing is perfect. You'll get to the top of the hill when you get there, using whatever means works for you. You won't be alone there. And the view will be breathtaking.

Julia (Julie) Erickson is a career and job search coach, blogger and writer. She is a subject matter expert on career management, the non-profit sector and a wide range of business leadership and management areas. Julie specializes in supporting people to find their "right fit" work—their individual paths to happiness and fulfillment in their work lives. Through coaching, teaching and writing, she enables people to pursue their dreams and passions, develop leadership ability, effectively market themselves, improve communication and interpersonal skills and make fulfilling work and career transitions. Julie is especially expert at helping people zero in on their "core value proposition" and effectively market themselves to employers and customers. Since 2008, she has helped more than a thousand people on their paths to their "right fit" work.

During her twenty-five years in New York City's nonprofit and public service sector, Julie raised more than one-hundred million dollars—much of it from individuals and through direct marketing. She led City Harvest for eleven years, and also led Bette Midler's New York Restoration Project. She exponentially increased City Harvest's impact and visibility, making City Harvest a household word for fighting hunger in New York City. Julie is most proud of shifting from delivering seventy-five percent baked goods out of four-and-a-half million pounds of food to delivering two-thirds fresh produce out of twenty-five million pounds of food delivered each year to nonprofits. Julie became expert at all things workforce while leading public/ private Initiatives at the New York City Department of Employment during the Dinkins administration. She honed her management skills at the Community Service Society of New York and began her fundraising career at a community development organization in the South Bronx.

Julie is a graduate of Smith College and has an MBA in leadership from New York Institute of Technology. She did graduate work in political theory at the University of Wisconsin-Madison and got specialized training at Columbia University's Institute for Non-Profit Management and NYU's Wagner School. Among her numerous awards are the James Beard Foundation's 2003 Humanitarian of the Year and Woman's Day *magazine's 2002 "Women Who Inspire Us." She is the author of* Your Right Fit Job: Guide to Getting Work You Really Love. *Connect with Julie at www.MyRightFitJob.com.*

Monika Jiang, MD

YOUR BODY IS THE FOUNDATION FOR YOUR SUCCESS

Transformation begins with your body. If you want to make a positive change in anything—career, finances, relationships, business, or mental or physical health—the easiest way to achieve that goal is to work on your body first. Without a solid body foundation any change or progress will break down sooner or later; or worse, you'll burn out and stop progressing altogether. When your body functions properly, other changes are much easier to make. Everything falls into place.

As a medical doctor specializing in general medicine and Chinese medicine, I know all too well that we can't expect our bodies, minds and souls to function properly if we don't care about basic nutrition and lifestyle principles. And yet, I forgot to apply those principles in my own life, for my own body. As I would discover later, I didn't really have the right training to know the *correct* key principles.

In 2011 I began an incredibly journey of self-development with New Peaks (formerly Peak Potentials), which lead to courses in London, all over Europe, and finally ended in Malaysia. On the road and especially by the Enlightened Warrior Camp, I had started to feel and think differently.

I had been involved with a nutritional supplements company for a few years and a friend convinced me to come with them to the United States for the company's convention. When I arrived, I learned about their new "Transformation Program," which promised, "Give us thirteen weeks and we give you a new life!" I thought, *That's a typical American slogan; not humble, not realistic at all.*

However, since I am a doctor and I love my patients, I decided to go into the program to research and experience its effectiveness in case it would be useful for my patients. I told myself, "I'm just doing this for scientific reasons, not because I need to do this for myself, not at all...."

As a doctor, I always focused first on my patients and fighting disease. But I lost myself on that path—I lost life balance and self-awareness, which showed in the extra weight I had been carrying around since the birth of my daughter. I had done what most self-

I went back to work after four weeks and forgot about my own needs.

employed people do after they have kids: I went back to work after four weeks and forgot about my own needs since I was busy trying to balance professional and family life.

I had a blind spot about my own body and my own wellness and no idea how bad it had gotten. When it was time to define my starting point, which meant photos and measurements, I was shocked. I had been carrying around an extra thirty pounds for nine years and never realized it! I had lost awareness about what I ate and what was good for me, and had completely given up on playing sports, as so many people do. I thought, *I didn't need to do this program for scientific reasons; I definitely needed to do this for myself!*

In the beginning, I didn't trust the program or believe in my own success, so I played safe and set a low goal: fourteen pounds in twelve weeks. I thought it would be pretty incredible to lose that much weight in twelve weeks. I started the program in Germany with my coach in the States. In the beginning, I felt flat and had no energy. Then, every week I felt more alive. Midway through the program I had already almost reached my first weight loss goal. So I set a higher goal. I felt more confident and realized the power of the strategy.

With the support of coaching and the right strategy, you can reach goals you couldn't even *imagine* in the beginning. At the end of the program I was back to the best shape of my life. I felt exactly as I did when I was twenty-two years old: young and dynamic, with the same weight and same endless energy. I had learned how

---

Every week I felt more alive.

---

to master my metabolism, enjoy this new healthy lifestyle and have seemingly endless energy. And at the same time I started to see how I could achieve other goals not related to my body—financial and business and career goals—using the strategies of transformation coaching and applying it to all areas of my life. With my body functioning optimally again, everything seemed so easy and new possibilities opened up.

I knew that this coaching with the right system had made all the difference for my success. My coach helped me to see my blind spots, and I learned some of the foods that I—a trained doctor— had thought were healthy really were part of my former problem. Because I wanted more people to benefit from the great power and possibilities of this coaching program, I began coaching other people who wanted to transform their bodies and reset to a better lifestyle or just lose weight and get fit and healthy and live in their power.

As is true for many working mothers, my client Stefanie was overwhelmed with multitasking and stressed by the pressures of having enough time for her kids and her work. She had been overweight for five years, since her last pregnancy. Losing weight was a big issue for her and a constant source of stress. She had tried many diets and never succeeded.

With me as her coach, Stefanie learned a lot about regularity, the rhythm of her body, what to eat and when to eat it, and how to integrate her new healthy lifestyle into her work and family life. She also learned the basic influencing factors of fat-burning and weight management. She lost a few pounds in the first two weeks, and even more importantly, her mood was more balanced. Week by week she became less stressed and had much more energy. She enjoyed her new lifestyle and was more relaxed about her weight goals.

Four weeks into the program, Stefanie's coworkers started asking her, "What are you doing? You look so good, but you can't be dieting, because you're not stressed out about food."

Before the end of the program, she had reached her personal goal of losing twenty pounds in twelve weeks. She felt great and had totally embraced her new lifestyle of fitness and vitality. She will keep this for the rest of her life, since it makes her feel so great. She knew she'd never have to worry about food or weight again.

It may have seemed she had succeeded in a weight loss program, but truly, she had achieved freedom from the stresses of her life and a lot of her worries and mood swings. It was a true transformation.

Another one of my clients came to me fearing if he did not make a change that year, the year he turned fifty, he would die of a heart attack. Uwe had overcome cancer years before and since then he had a fear of dying due to his stress at work and poor lifestyle habits. He was overworked, never worked out and did not eat well. To make it worse, he had set a goal of running a half-marathon before his fiftieth birthday. After his birthday passed and he still hadn't attempted any change, he realized he couldn't make the shift on his own.

Uwe began his transformation one week before Christmas. It was easy to get him back into his running shoes and on the road. What was *not* so easy was to get him to correct the destructive lifestyle he had slipped into due to his job: a lot of late-night business dinners, travel, no regular schedule and a daily consumption of red wine. I helped Uwe find his blind spots, and after just two weeks he could already see results. He was fired up! He made good progress and started changing his habits, one by one. I showed him how to adjust the program and its principles to his traveling schedule and work appointments and thereby gain consistency.

By the end of the program, Uwe was back to the shape he had been in fifteen years ago. He felt great, went for a run daily and, when he was at home, prepared healthy meals rather than going out to eat, much to the delight of his wife. He pulled out his old favorite jeans and they fit, and he looked even better in a closely

---

*Your body is the best foundation
for your success.*

---

tailored buisiness suit. But the real transformation was that Uwe no longer felt held back by his cancer story and he no longer feared death. He now knew how to take care of his body and understood its power of self-healing given the right nutrients and training. With certainty that he could maintain his healthy lifestyle, Uwe began to see that other goals were possible and he began making plans for his future.

It is amazing how much you can change by working intensely on your body, focusing on nutrition, training and lifestyle and on you as your source of power. When you fix what your body needs first and fuel it with the right nutrients, training and rest, you make a quantum leap in energy, which makes it so much easier to pursue your goals. Your mind gets sharper, more alert, so you improve your ability to tap into what you really want out of life and have the energy to go and get it. And once your health and body are balanced and in their prime, you can easily imagine accomplishing transformations in other areas as well.

Working with a coach accelerates the process of transformation by leaps and makes it much easier: no detours, no long-lasting self-sabotage. As a medical doctor, I was expected to work independently; coaching seemed like a strange idea. But I came to discover—through my own journey and that of my coaching clients—that personal one-on-one support can help you make real change in a very short time. In fact, it is almost the only way to make massive changes in an elegant, almost painless way. My life is forever changed thanks to the guidance of my coach and the principles I learned, and I've seen impressive changes in my own clients. I've seen people completely change their body shapes in just three months and, what is even more impressive, completely change their lifestyles, energies and how they stand in life.

Working with a coach can transform your life. A coach can show you your blind spots and help you overcome them. Your coach believes in you more than you believe in yourself. And your coach knows the recipe for success: the key skills, the secrets of metabolism, what to do and what to avoid. Step by step, week by week, your coach helps you make the "impossible" possible and achieve your dreams.

Your body is the best foundation for your success. Heart-centered transformation must include nourishing your heart, learning to love yourself and treating your body accordingly. You can't have a fulfilled life if your brain is malnourished, if you lack amino acids or omega-3, if your hormones are off or if your organs don't function well due to slow intoxication. Your body, mind and heart work according to the kind of nourishment they get. In my experience, quite a lot of "mental" or "psychological" problems are just the manifestation of bad lifestyle habits, harmful diet and lack of exercise.

Wherever you come from, whatever worked or did not work for you before and whatever stories you've told yourself about your ability or inability to change, you can transform your life one-hundred percent once you have the right tools and techniques, once you know what to do, step by step. Your journey begins with a healthy body and a coach to guide you on the path to transformation. Start with your body and then listen to your heart. The rest will easily follow and take you to your fullest successes.

Monika Jiang, MD, is in private practice in Weinheim, Germany with an emphasis on traditional Chinese medicine, hypnotherapy and naturopathy. She combines Western and Chinese modalities, as well as her training as a coach, to help her clients and patients achieve health and happiness. Her process begins with the thirteen-week body transformation program that dramatically changed her life and the lives of hundreds of others for the better. She specializes in training other coaches to make this program available to as many people as possible.

Monika earned her medical degree from the University of Heidelberg and passed her state medical exams in 1993. In that same year she began her education in Chinese medicine, studying Qi Gong, an ancient method of achieving optimal health that involves specific techniques for breathing, physical postures and intention. She went on to study chirotherapy, hypnotherapy, Chinese herbology and feng-shui.

In 1997, Monika earned a Diploma of Chinese Herbology from the Academy of Chinese Healing Arts in Winterthur, Switzerland. In 2000 she was approved by the German Society of Chan Mi Gong to teach Qi Gong and began teaching at the Tai Jiang Centrum. She received her certification in medical and psychotherapeutical hypnosis in 2003 and in 2005 became a specialist in general medicine.

Monika has been a health transformation and lifestyle coach since 2012, training with Peak Potentials, Unicity and Blair Singer. She is the author of "Chan Mi Gong: Durch Einen Gestärkten Rücken zu Innerer Harmonie." *She works with clients all over the world. Connect with Monika at her English website www.TransformToPrime.com.*

Julie Simard

To Begin Again

I am a warrior with a butterfly's heart.

In 2012 I took a bus to New York City to spend the weekend with my friend Stephan and his wife, Hilary. Earlier that year I started having mobility issues due to multiple sclerosis (MS), but as is usually my way, I let nothing hold me back. Having just lost my best friend Manon to lung cancer, I needed space to breathe. I needed new air. I needed to be with my old friend.

Just before my trip, I had a stupid accident in the sauna of a spa: I slipped on a step and badly hurt my left foot. Though it was just an accident, it seemed like the last straw in a series of profound losses: my husband, my career in publishing and television, my freedom to move as I pleased. *How long will this go on?* I wondered.

Still, I wanted to visit Stephan, so with a gray astronaut boot on my left foot, I set out on the bus from Montreal to New York. I sat in the front row with my leg up on the seat in front of me; my body was in pain from walking and standing in long lines. Stephan came to pick me up at the bus station in his car, and we had a lovely time. Stephan and Hilary showed me the best sites, day and night.

At the Guggenheim Museum, Stephan pushed me in a wheelchair so I could enjoy the visit without experiencing pain. I had never used such equipment before. I am very proud, and would not even accept the use of a walking stick or a handicap sticker for parking my car. I didn't want anyone to know about my challenges. With respect to my MS, I lived by these mottos: "It doesn't show, so don't let it show," "No one has to know," and "It's none of their business."

Still, I trusted Stephan completely. As he wheeled me around the museum, the unusual spiralled floors rolled out before us like a magic carpet. We nourished our minds and souls, having fun as we did when we were teenagers. In that moment I knew MS would

---

I didn't want anyone to know about my challenges.

---

not deter me from my dreams, goals or projects. It would not deter me from living my life!

I was diagnosed with MS in 2006. I was expecting the diagnosis, having had two episodes in three months: an optic neuritis in my right eye and major numbness in my right leg. I was prepared, but when the neurologist gave me my prognosis, I was distracted and profoundly hurt. Losing a part of your natural gift is difficult to recover from. I couldn't accept it. I wondered, *Will I now walk on thin ice until the next fall?* The sword of Damocles was over my head.

My illness scares people, and many women diagnosed with MS are lonely and depressed. I didn't want that for myself or for my family. I am alive and kicking. I want to have fun with my two beautiful sons—my *raison d'être*—to share great times with them and guide them.

We all have handicaps. Some are linked with the misunderstanding of foreign languages or cultures. Some arise with regard to political issues. Some have physical handicaps, or emotional challenges or crises of the spirit. My interest is to understand, to go past preconceived notions of what is possible, past limitations, past judgments, and to help people with MS and other handicaps so they can live with dignity and respect.

I used to say, "Just touch me, you'll have a blessing! I was born at Sainte-Anne-De-Beaupré." The basilica in my hometown was known as a place for miracles. When I got my vision back, it certainly seemed like a miracle! It seemed as though I was helping people with MS to hear that the sentence of loss of vision need not be permanent. I was a channel to a cure, to happiness, to energy and to love.

It was devastating when my illness forced me to leave my position in publishing, but now I look back over the triumphs and the achievements with reverence. The remarkable stories I helped birth, the effusive praise from authors I worked with, calling me an "inspirational force" and a "lover of life" fortified me as I ventured out onto a new journey. I thought, *I still have a voice. I have light to share, values to share. Begin again.*

Today, MS is a transformative tool. I have used this experience to broaden my horizons, to find better things for me. I have gone

I have gone beyond the path I once loved.

beyond the path I once loved, the career I mastered. I am no longer superwoman, but I am someone new. This warrior has a transformative heart, a butterfly's heart. I glorify my true colors.

I still cherish my field of communications, but being a TV director and editor in the French market limited me in the worldwide spectrum. So, I took a year to study and learn crucial marketing and selling strategies. Now, I collaborate with key influencers aligned with my expertise and vision. Like my father and grandfather before me, I am an entrepreneur. Being a communications expert, I decided it was time to master finance and to become a dedicated reporter. I help bring to the world the stories that can make a difference.

My mission now is to create a totally free virtual community website to solve all isolation problems generated by all handicaps, helping those who need the best medication for the rest of their life so they can feel better every day, so they are able to move without assistance, with flexibility, with choice of location and so they can enjoy life more! With my background as a media producer and director, having worked with more than fifteen hundred celebrities in over ten years, I know what it takes to get attention from all types of media. As a content expert, I have built a solid team of

---

I am intent on bouncing back.

---

renowned partners and "geeks" to help create a digital business platform. I believe in action! I want to educate and experience a great new day. I devote myself with clear commitments; my heart-centered business is here to change mentalities, perceptions and reactions.

Often, people talk about not wasting time on those in need. I do not like this negative approach. I prefer to work with my chi, to diminish my stress, raise my concentration abilities and my overall well-being. I take a step back to re-center and focus my energy. I am intent on bouncing back, becoming more alert, agile and full of laughter. I plan to re-learn how to walk without a limp, maybe even run!

I practice walking to fulfill another goal: to trek to the top of Mount Everest accompanied by women with MS, scientists and a camera crew to document the experience and raise awareness about MS. I visualize this goal every day. I see the team meeting the citizens of the world, from Nepal, to India, to China and Tibet. I see the Dalai Lama joining us on our trek. I see China supporting our goal. And when I talk about my project with people who share my values, I get the sense that my idea is a given, destined, powerful. I see it in the shining eyes of the people who listen.

I need a stronger pace, a stronger walk. But I will do the Everest challenge. Will you accompany me?

Last summer I had a small episode with MS that set me back. I had no sensation in my right foot. I love mountains, and I decided to try to walk the mountains with resources and trekking picks.

I knew it would be a test to measure my capacity. What I learned there, and what I felt there, was unbelievable.

We were four teams on a trail with five stops at Whistler, near Vancouver. My body felt like an older woman's body. After twenty minutes of exercise, my muscles and my nerves were shaky until I rested. My reflexes would not respond correctly at all times, so I had to be careful when executing movements on the mountain. I kept saying to myself, *One step at a time.* I got hurt and couldn't go all the way to the top, but three hikers stayed with me to help. They helped me walk in the dangerous zones. They made me feel special, saying I inspired them with my courage, my bravery and my happiness.

My body and soul are at the mercy of science. I hope to make a lot of money that serves my causes well, and for the first time, give myself the freedom to find peace and love. I am still vulnerable, but so what? I am curious and I feel the clock ticking. The pressure of time slipping by inspires me to stay open-minded and to take action. The focus on health and exercise and my new flow to reactivate, that is how I can feel better. I'd better watch my nutrition!

There is always a way, if you listen to your heart. You see the museum from a wheelchair—does it matter? You walk carefully and slowly up the mountain—does it matter? You need extra time due to a handicap—does it matter? Evolve. Evolve. Be open, share the good vibes and believe in dreams.

Julie Simard is a bilingual manager, publisher, producer and writer, with more than twenty years of experience in production and communications. She has vast expertise in project development and execution of content for print and online media and television. Known for her ability to adapt, lead and work under pressure, Julie has worked with a variety of groups. She has edited many books and she has brought many video projects to market. Connect with Julie at www.YueliProductions.com.

Michael Silvers

WILLING TO TAKE THE RISK

One of my favorite success stories is about the transcontinental railroad, the rail system that stretched from coast to coast and established America's infrastructure for the future. If you grew up in the United States, you may remember learning about it in school. What may not have hit home when you were cracking that American History textbook was the great lesson from that story.

Yes, the achievement was remarkable, but the important point of that endeavor was not the dream itself, but how that "impossible" dream was achieved. Tycoons, politicians, inventors—everyone with a vested interest had been trying to come up with a way to build a rail system to the West Coast since the dawn of the steam locomotive in 1830. The six-month trip by wagon was treacherous and expensive, and the only other way to reach California was to travel by ship all the way around the continent of South America. Despite the great need for a railroad that would connect the westernmost stop in Nebraska to the port cities of the coast, no one could agree on a route or the best way to lay track through mountains, across streams and through dangerous territories.

It wasn't until President Abraham Lincoln signed the Pacific Railroad Act into law in 1862 that work began Two companies— Union Pacific Railroad and Central Pacific Railroad Company—

would be in a race to the finish. The only plan the two companies had was they would start at opposite ends and meet somewhere in the middle.

It was a race to see which company could lay track faster. Central Pacific started in Sacramento and worked its way through the Sierra Nevada Mountains, blasting dynamite through granite as they went. Union Pacific started in Nebraska. They didn't know how to get where they were going, or where their next dime of funding was coming from. But they knew which direction to go

---

The failure I experienced had been
about fear of moving forward.

---

and they had an idea of where they would end up. They picked a location as a goal and built the track to get there. Then they picked the next location, and the next, and the next. When they encountered obstacles, they went around, under or through—whatever it took to get to the next stop.

Foot by foot, mile by mile, tens of thousands of workers laid track until President Ulysses S. Grant informed the two companies that they would have to decide where they would meet and connect the two rail systems. Six years after they began building the railroad, the final spike—the "golden spike"—was driven in Utah, not far from the Great Salt Lake.

The journey to build the country's rail system was not without tragedy. It is beyond the scope of this chapter to discuss the political, social and ethical events that mark the history of how the transcontinental railroad came to be. Still, the success of the endeavor is remarkable. When both companies laid their first track, they had no idea how to get where they were going or what obstacles they would face. The path didn't matter—they knew the end result, they believed they could do it and they just got started.

For the past twenty years, I have developed training and coaching programs for personal and professional development. It has provided me the great privilege to meet a lot of good people with great ideas who work hard at bringing these ideas to fruition. And, simply stated, one of two paths are taken. The people who simplify their strategic processes and are willing to take a chance, accepting the element of risk that comes with every step forward, succeed beautifully. Those who complicate their approach get stuck. Rather than undivided focus on the goal, avoiding risk becomes the driving factor. While risk avoidance can be prudent, it is the getting stuck in it that stops people in their tracks.

Early in my career, I found myself promoted into a new leadership position for a large multi-national company. I was enthusiastic about the work, but feared making mistakes. While the vision was clear, company ethos had little tolerance for risk and the path forward found itself shackled to the weight of time

---

Leadership is about a willingness to get people where they want to go.

---

and energy spent avoiding the "what if's" of failure. I jumped on that train. Needed change didn't happen. The decision-making process suffered, not for lack of vision, but for an inability to pull the trigger.

When you are at your lowest point, in the darkest of the dark, all you need is a ray of light to show you the way up. For me, that ray of light was a quote from General Colin Powell I happened to come across, a quote that literally blinded me with its powerful message: "Great leaders are almost always great simplifiers, who can cut through argument, debate and doubt to offer a solution everybody can understand."

I came to realize that failure wasn't a complex set of circumstances. At its very core, the failure I experienced had been about fear of moving forward. Success, then, does not rely on a complex set of circumstances. Rather, it absolutely requires that I am willing to move forward toward the place I say I want to go. Period!

Leadership is about a willingness to get people where they want to go. I don't need to know every step in advance. I do need to know what my clients need and sometimes what they want. Once I'm sure of the result they desire, I motivate my team and my clients to begin walking forward, foot by foot, mile by mile, until they drive their versions of the golden spike right into the ground and change their worlds forever.

When I build a training program for New Peaks™, I have the concept of what the student wants and where they want to go. I create a working framework that leads them from Point A to Point B. Then we launch! We start by moving forward. Movement builds

---

Do the next thing, wait for feedback,
and then do the next thing.

---

momentum. Momentum makes movement easier. We anticipate feedback and remain nimble, ready to respond with the course corrections that are part of every journey forward.

When people fail to get results from a personal development program it is because the program was too complicated or their fear (perceived obstacles) blocked the launch. Failure to launch is almost always tied to over-complication. When the steps are simple and get you to the next, you are more likely to *take* that first step. "Next" doesn't seem so far away. It's a few feet down the road or track, not all the way to the California coast! You're still taking a risk on your big goal, but the next step is just a step.

The more you simplify your approach to achieving anything, the closer you remain to true success. When we complicate the message, we put obstacles and barriers in place and we get stuck in our heads trying to solve problems. We forget the heart, the driving force behind the goal, the dream that is our vision, and we get caught in fear.

I had a client who was building a new marketing business. She proudly presented her business plan, the product of over six months of hard work and fine tuning. The problem? She had yet to pick up the phone and contact prospective clients. She had instead spent time creating plans and processes for every possible objection she might encounter. Dead in her tracks. We started with a new plan. Goal: contact one new potential client per week. Actions: play music that inspires, write a script (short), pick up the phone. Achieving her goal was tied to actions, not on whether prospective clients said yes or no. Simple step. Within a year she was the top producer for her company.

When you have one task for the day, and you take a chance and complete it, that triggers your brain to think "wow, I had a success!" Celebrate! Celebrating success is vital as it powerfully impacts how we think and feel about ourselves. We're newly motivated to stay the course. Goal-Action-Success-Celebration!

Realizing seemingly impossible dreams is not out of your reach. Re-tool your own strategic processes for launching your own venture. Get total clarity about the result you wish to achieve and then simplify the approach so you are focused only on the next step, not on potential obstacles or challenges.

Do the next thing, wait for feedback, and then do the next thing. Lay your track foot by foot, mile by mile, and before you know it, you'll have your own "transcontinental railroad." Begin today. Do one simple thing toward your goal in the next twenty-four hours. Take one step, lay one piece of track, take one chance. Greatness awaits those who are willing to take the risk!

Michael Silvers is a trainer and director of coaching for New Peaks™ and is responsible for developing and coordinating the company's training and coaching programs in the United States and Canada. Michael's clear and consistent strategic and tactical direction has been key to supporting the rapid growth of New Peaks, recruiting and training New Peaks coaches and continually designing and developing new trainings, coaching models and techniques. As director and trainer, Michael has excelled in leading and developing teams and individuals to achieve peak performance and has helped tens of thousands of individuals create the wealth and engineer the lifestyles they truly desire. He has also developed and managed an interactive website to help provide an online community and support for New Peaks clients worldwide.

Michael's career and experience span a variety of professional roles over the last twenty years that have consistently focused on the development of personal and professional achievement. He earned a Master's degree in clinical psychology in 1990 and is a master trainer and practitioner of neuro-linguistic programming. Connect with Michael at www.NewPeaks.com.

Thorsten Bonn

Be the Creator of Tomorrow

"Let's get one thing out of the way first and foremost: I need you to be okay with this becoming a complete failure."

These are not the words you want to hear when you're trying to decide if you want to become an entrepreneur. After five years working for a software company serving the auction industry, I had been given the opportunity to take over the business—a business that had just lost its major trade partner. My old boss was giving me a chance to take over the company, start over with our few other clients and try to make a go of it.

I was facing the biggest challenge of my life thus far. Should I take on the risk with expenses, employees and an uncertain future? In my decision process, I had access to a coach, Angela, who helped me to see things from different angles. I was surprised she wanted me to even consider failure, let alone embrace it. Angela went on to say, "You cannot go forward with confidence and succeed in this if you don't right here, and right now, accept and make peace with the possibility that you might fail."

"Isn't that a very negative view?" I asked.

"No," she replied. "If you accept that the business could fail, then you don't have that worry hanging over you every day when you come to the office. You can make decisions more freely. You can move forward and think, 'If we fail, we fail.' You can focus on building the company, rather than saving it from a potential negative outcome."

Everyone—my girlfriend, my parents, most of my friends—said I shouldn't take on the financial investment and responsibility of owning the company and that I should find a real "job."

It wasn't the first time I had faced opposition from my parents. I'm sort of the black sheep because, aside from my grandfather Alfred, I'm the only entrepreneur in a family of academics. Most of them were in government research or the education system,

I hadn't intended to be the person at the helm.

which meant they had a secure job, weeks of paid vacation, good benefits and a pension. It also meant they contended with fairly rigid structures. I didn't yet know why or how, but I knew very early on in life that I wanted to walk a different path.

Despite my parents' urging to follow in their footsteps, I had decided to do my own thing. At the end of high school I had no idea what I wanted to do in my university life. I thought, *I'll get a degree and see what happens after that.* Eventually, I went to work for a publicly traded software company and I enjoyed that job.

Now I was facing taking over a company with a mountain of responsibilities and challenges to face, and I had no real prior business experience other than what I learned from books at university. I hadn't intended to be the person at the helm. When we heard the news that we had lost our major trade partner, our former boss explained that we would have to develop our software so we could retain our smaller clients, but we may still have to shut down.

"There's still value in this business. Let's see if we can sell it," he said.

We knocked on a few doors and nobody was interested in the company at the price we asked. Then our former boss asked my immediate superior at the company if he was interested in buying the company and taking it over; he too declined.

When it looked as though we had no other options and would have to close the company, he said, "Let's give Thorsten a chance."

The deal was, he would give me an opportunity to make a go of it, but we would have to generate our own revenue and carry all the expenses of the complete company without any help to be expected from any bank or outside source. I thought about the risk, the responsibility and my parent's objections. It would take a tremendous effort to build the company up, and I had a steep learning curve. I felt sick to my stomach and worried up to the point where I had not slept well, if at all, for weeks.

Then I talked to my coach. Her advice about accepting failure hit home. It was my biggest "a-ha!" moment.

Her words had lifted a weight off my shoulders. I could fail, yes. But I would survive. The worst-case scenario was something I could manage, which is really what we're worried about when we fear failure. I said, "You know what, that's it, I'm doing this."

I still had the same pessimists around me and the same conditions. I had no idea where the money was coming from and what things would look like tomorrow, or whether my key team members would trust my leadership, but I was going for it. We

> **I had no idea where the money
> was coming from.**

took it a day at a time. I borrowed some money privately, and we started over. We started with zero revenue and we had no idea where the next rent, utility or payroll money would come from. It was a very tough year.

Nobody thought we would make it. Most months we scraped by, and some days we had so little money and so few prospects that my faith was really stretched. It was liberating to follow my heart and not my brain when I was making business decisions. While that meant setting aside logic and sometimes taking a higher risk, it also was, and still is, one of the cornerstones of why our business succeeds and grows, because the payoffs are much bigger as well and the risk is predominantly created from a headspace decision.

In the difficult times, I thought about my grandfather Alfred. I vaguely remembered him; he passed away when I was three years old. Alfred didn't fit the family mold because, after returning to Mannheim, Germany, from serving in World War II and being in French captivity, he decided to forego government work and become an electrician in business for himself.

When Alfred started out he had little but a bicycle and his business license, as well as a few tools for his electrical work. The years of rebuilding after the war were hard on many people, so he would go around Mannheim on a bicycle and, when he saw that people were standing inside the ruins of their former houses, he would offer his services when they started to rebuild.

Alfred's little business grew over the years, and when he retired, he had a respectable company that was the main supplier

You don't want your life to happen to you.
You want to be the creator of tomorrow.

of electrical services in a mid-sized German city. Whenever a developer put up a new building, he would try to purchase a unit.

Although my grandmother Pia had wanted him to find government work, in hindsight she was very proud of his achievements. And she realized the government pension she had wanted all along would not have been enough to live on. However, because of my grandfather's foresight, she was able to live well on the rental income from the properties he'd purchased over the years.

She once told me, "You know what? If your grandfather didn't have such vision I would be a poor woman today."

As I thought back on all of the stories my grandmother told me about Alfred, I realized I *was* following in my family's footsteps—I was like Alfred. Not just because he bucked the family tradition and became an entrepreneur, but because he had *foresight*. He had vision. He made his ideas work in his mind first and then he executed them. He was the creator of his tomorrow.

We stayed the course. By the end of the second year, it was clear we had a viable company. We had turned it around. Six years later, we are one of the most successful players in the marketplace, with more than a thousand clients worldwide.

One of the many things that has given us an early edge in our marketplace is willingness to think outside the box. Each client and partner has different needs and expectations, and every business is at a different stage. It rarely makes sense to offer one solution to all clients. Instead we are a bespoke service provider building our offerings around their needs at their price points. It means we sometimes make less money up front, but we gain a trusted partnership and priceless loyalty for many years that always pays off higher in the long run.

Whether we focus on it or not, we are always creating the next second, the next minute and the next hour. Most people are living by default, reacting to a "reality," and they always get the same outcome because they more or less remain in the same mind frame. When we focus our energy on avoiding failure, we create a tomorrow that is at best safe and unfulfilling, and at worst attracts the very failure we fear the most.

You don't want your life to happen to you. You want to be the creator of tomorrow. Over the years I've come to realize that vision and perspective go hand in hand. Perspective has been the deciding factor in so many of the successful ventures in my life. You can choose to see and focus on what is, commonly and mistakenly referred to "reality" or choose to see what could be and what you want and then make it so.

Success is living on your terms. To me it simply means being in a position to do what you want, when you want and with whom you want to do it. It doesn't have to be about accumulating money or running a big company; it doesn't have to be living up to a family legacy you *don't want*.

Failure happens. It might happen to you. But would you really *be* a failure if it did? Not in my opinion. "Failure" is a learning experience on your way to the next major success. If you wake up in the morning and you feel as if you're doing something worthwhile, something that brings you joy and pleasure, to me, you are a successful person.

Thorsten Bonn grew up in Germany in a family of academics, yet after graduating from high school, he opted to forge his own way and found a civil service placement, which allowed him to work in the foreign relations department of the federal government. Thorsten attended the University of British Columbia in Vancouver. His business degree, which he completed with a marketing designation, landed him his first job at a publicly traded auction company. He worked as an employee there for five years before the company changed its structure and he got the opportunity to become an entrepreneur. Connect with Thorsten at www.iCollector.com.

Helma Christiane Bloomberg

Together We Can

One morning thirty-six years ago, I woke up in my beautiful home in Beverly Hills next to a husband who loved and spoiled me. My plans for the day included playing tennis on our private court, then enjoying lunch with my girlfriends and doing a little shopping. I drove a big car, traveled the world and wanted for nothing. That morning, despite my gratitude for my many blessings, I looked out the window at the bright California sun rising and asked myself, "Is that all there is?"

I wonder if you too have had moments like this, moments where you asked yourself, "Is that all there is?" Have you looked around at the life you are living, the life you built, and longed for deeper meaning and contribution and to leave a lasting legacy?

I was born in Berlin, Germany a few months after the end of the Second World War. Six months earlier, in May, as the western Allies bombarded the city, my Catholic parents had tried to flee and escape the blockade. During their attempted escape, however, my father was tragically killed by shrapnel and bled to death in my mother's arms. My pregnant mother then returned to the city, and I was thereafter born.

As a young child in a devastated country, I suffered from typhus and nearly died. Berlin had a poor, unhealthy food supply—milk, for example, was often contaminated. I felt the horrible aftermath of war—its displacement and dislocation—and it afflicted my family. The tragedy of war had forced three generations of my family into Berlin when it had not been home to any of us.

My mother re-married, to a Lutheran man. I first became fascinated with the United States when one of my teachers in Germany, Director Luther, inspired us with wonderful stories about Americans. His warm feelings for America were ironic because American soldiers had occupied his home in Germany during the war. Rather than share horror stories, Director Luther

My father was tragically killed by shrapnel.

spoke warmly about the American soldiers and the way they treated his family so well. Director Luther's experience with the American occupation influenced my optimism; it planted a seed in my mind and heart that ethnic or national barriers—ostensibly insurmountable—may be overcome.

I moved to the United States in 1966, settled in Palm Springs, California, attended college and eventually met my husband who was still finishing his residency training at UCLA Medical Center. He was a doctor—a surgeon—and his family was Jewish. We raised two children in the predominantly Jewish-American community of Beverly Hills. I constantly faced questions in the community at-large about my relationship to Nazi Germany. People assumed I was a Nazi sympathizer even though I had been born after the war and even though my family, along with others, had been forced to leave Switzerland for re-settlement in the destroyed Germany.

My own perspective emerged from the particular circumstances of my life and its history. I see both the darkness and the light of our present civilization because I have intimate experience with the greatest horrors as well as the most fortunate opportunities of my generation. It would have been all too easy to have allowed the trappings of wealth to overshadow my unique perspective and my desire to give and contribute to the world.

After that morning of revelation I couldn't shake the feeling that life was meant for a greater purpose. *Of course that's not all there is to life!* When I grew up in Berlin and later in Munich my family was part of the art world. On a yearly basis my parents exhibited with local and global fine art and antique dealers in the House of Arts by the Englisher Garten in Munich. We lived in the heart of Munich. The once-destroyed city and opera house had been rebuilt, the visual and performing arts started to thrive again as well, and as a family we eagerly participated in the progress.

After moving to the United States, with perseverance and determination, both my husband and I working very hard, together we eventually reached the pinnacle of success, and it was a natural decision for me to begin my journey of philanthropy by joining the Los Angeles Ballet Guild. Later I served on the Board, then the

For nearly forty years I have worked as an agent for positive transformation.

Los Angeles Opera Board, was a major donor to the Los Angeles Library Foundation and served as director on the Beverly Hills Education Foundation so I could personally foster the education of our two daughters whom we loved, cherished and adored.

In the coming years I organized and raised funds for charity sports tournaments, both in the field of tennis and dressage. I was an equestrienne, as were our two daughters, Stephanie and Alanna. One of my daughters was a five-time World Champion in the hunter jumper circuit in Fort Worth, Texas; the other attended Vassar College and earned a master's degree in psychology. Together with my daughters and the assistance of the entire Hanson Dam Equestrian Center we put on a sports tournament to raise funds for our friend Heather Bender to send her to the Olympic tryouts in St. Louis, Missouri.

In the arts, I was personally responsible for Los Angeles Opera's young artists to be able to showcase their talent at the Beverly Hills Summer Arts Festival for eight consecutive years, with an attendance of well over a thousand spectators every year. My work embraced hosting young artists in the visual and the performing arts at my home, raising money for their tuition, showcasing their talents and facilitating global connections. My work was highly gratifying. I woke up each morning inspired and full of passion. Slowly, with determination and joy, I built a legacy—a legacy of generosity.

For nearly forty years I have worked as an agent for positive transformation. The horrors of my childhood and the optimism of Director Luther remained influences as I strove to raise funds and awareness to improve the lives of people globally. I founded the International Society of Cultural Ambassadors. Among its pursuits, this society and its friends supported the education of

*We must always be prepared to
defend human rights fiercely.*

meritorious young artists by connecting them with schools in foreign countries to hone their skills, as well as by providing them with venues to showcase their talents and by assisting them, either at home or abroad, by making important connections for them.

My devoted commitment to exchange dialogue is evidenced by the work of the German-American Cultural Society, of which I served as a board member. The society worked to normalize German-Jewish relations. In 2008, along with Jimmy Delshad, the incoming Mayor of Beverly Hills, I was invited by Ambassador Elin Suleymanov to attend a Global Forum in Baku, Azerbaijan and there I enjoyed the distinct honor of sharing the podium with the First Lady of Azerbaijan, Madam Mehriban Aliyeva. I have since had the opportunity to take the podium in San Diego at Consular Corps events and was recently invited to address a Chamber of Commerce meeting in our beautiful state of Texas. The last two years have found me in Washington, D.C. on several occasions, and I am looking forward to being there again this fall participating in fundraising and cultural exchange events.

Over the course of my journey I have studied human civilization and the human condition looking for answers for real and lasting change. I've come to understand that our world is distinguished by stunning examples of cohesion and fragmentation, increasing order and rising chaos, persistent nationalism and emergent humanism, more secularism and more fundamentalisms.

Perhaps as human beings we must battle over limited, finite resources on this small planet. Or, perhaps humanity can escape the zero-sum game in which one party's victory must be another's loss. We surely know this about ourselves and our nature: Human beings are innocent, noble souls degraded by the offenses of civilization. And, we also contain a survival instinct that yearns for power. Both assessments of human nature are needed to accurately portray the full richness, the light and the dark sides, the yin and the yang of human experience.

I suggest that we must blend an unsentimental, stark realism with a genuine optimism. Too many are suffering, and we must always be prepared to defend human rights fiercely. I hope my words here echo the great insight of Albert Einstein when he said, "No problem may be solved at the same level of consciousness which created it." The problems are real, but so is our capacity to foster a greater and more generous consciousness to solve them.

My life was shaped by the great conflict of the twentieth century, and also by the hopeful movement of peoples and integration of cultures that it hastened. From my experiences, I understand that conflict is a necessary prerequisite for significant change—that, as awful as it may be, conflict stimulates growth. Frederick Douglass, the great nineteenth century American abolitionist, describes this dynamic most eloquently. In 1857, on the occasion of the abolition of slavery in the West Indies, Douglass said, "If there is no struggle, there is no progress. Those who… depreciate agitation are men who want crops without plowing up the ground. They want rain without thunder and lightning… They want the ocean without the awful roar of its many waters. This struggle may be a moral one or it may be a physical one… but it must be a struggle."

Each of us—life by life and day by day—can push through on a personal basis to make a difference. I think Churchill called it "soldiering on," and I've always been inspired by his phrase. Our new consciousness does not require the restructuring of the global order of nations or a new epoch of technology. An enlightened, humane way of thinking and acting is available to all of us, now.

Today, I share my expertise on building a legacy of generosity with individuals, groups and organizations large and small. I help successful CEOs and business leaders raise their company profiles and their profits by connecting them to causes that are personally and professionally rewarding. And I started my own foundation dedicated to fostering excellence in our young and upcoming generation in the performing and visual arts, science and sports. My renewed purpose is to give youth the support they need to thrive. It gives me such joy to see young people actualize their dream. It is both an honor and a pleasure to assist in making their journey to success a joyful and a happy one.

On a local level, in every small way, each of us must renew Gandhi's pledge "to be the change we want to see in the world." Where you see an opportunity to support early childhood education, embrace it. Where there's a spark to bring young people together in a multinational camp, ignite it. Where a community can afford the means to conserve resources, implement it. Where individuals commit violence, stop it. Where people speak out for freedom, protect it. Where students express their creativity, rejoice in it.

If you, too, have had a moment of wondering, "Is that all there is," I call on you to consider your own legacy. How will you make a difference in this world? How will you "soldier on," allowing past struggles to inform your unique offering for the world? How will you create opportunities for others you once wished you had?

For most of our lives we reach outward—we build our businesses, provide for our families, obtain a certain amount of visible success shown by our possessions, our titles and by the degrees we garnered along the way. But if you think deeply about your place in society, and in the universe, and if you ask yourself once more: "Is that all there is?" then with all my heart I invite you to reach inward and find within you the true center of the self.

Our time together is short, and not every day is going to offer us an opportunity to save someone's life, but every day we are given the chance to affect one. To quote Vince Lombardi: "The measure of who we are is what we do with what we have." I know that each and everyone of us can do something meaningful with what we have, and that together we truly can make a difference.

Helma Christiane Bloomberg inspires people to live their highest purpose by helping them create a legacy of generosity around their persona or their organizations. Through inspirational keynote presentations, Mrs. Bloomberg teaches and models transformational leadership. She guides people in designing an ideal life that matters through personal or corporate giving and by implementing her powerful tools for cultivating passion and generosity.

Mrs. Bloomberg has enjoyed a distinguished career of public service and philanthropy for organizations that promote the arts, science, athletics and cultural exchange. Her numerous pro bono activities seek to galvanize international goodwill and promote cultural awareness. To facilitate international commerce, she connects members of the diplomatic corps with American business leaders, while at the same time showcasing their cultures through the print media. Mrs. Bloomberg has been recognized by the Los Angeles Consular Corps for her outstanding devotion and invaluable contributions to the diplomatic corps as International Liaison. In 2004, the South East Symphony named her as one of Beverly Hills' "Most Exciting Women." As a champion of the arts, Mrs. Bloomberg has served on the boards of the Los Angeles Opera Company and the Los Angeles Ballet Company. She is currently a supporter of the Kansas City Symphony and the Kansas City Lyric Opera. She has served on the Metropolitan Opera

National Council Auditions and was a National Council member. As a board member of the William Kapell Piano Foundation she commissioned works by young pianists and provided performance opportunities. Mrs. Bloomberg contributed funds and support for the Media Lounge at the Goethe Institute and the Zachary Auditions for young opera singers; she was a contributing member of the Wagner Society. On behalf of the Los Angeles Consular Corps and the Los Angeles Philharmonic, she has mobilized fund-raising initiatives and personally supported their events.

Mrs. Bloomberg treasures the friendship of the members of the Asian Ladies Circle of Los Angeles and provided aid to victims afflicted by the great tsunami of 2004. She served as Director of the Beverly Hills Education Foundation. In addition Mrs. Bloomberg was pleased to assist exceptional talent of an International Society of Cultural Ambassadors. The International Society and its benefactors promoted young artists by offering them performance opportunities, financial assistance and, with the help of the diplomatic corps, facilitated connections overseas. In return, the society encouraged these dedicated and gifted individuals to build bridges of friendship and to be emissaries of their skills and cultures.

Mrs. Bloomberg continues to devote time to cross-cultural dialogue by facilitating connections and by attending functions of the diplomatic corps both in Los Angeles and in Washington, D.C. On behalf of health and science philanthropies, Mrs. Bloomberg is particularly proud to have served as chair of a Cedars Sinai Medical Center's annual three-day event for diabetes which culminated in a televised "Legends of Tennis" match at the Playboy Mansion.

Mrs. Bloomberg is a sponsor of the Austrian-American Council West and of the Los Angeles-Berlin Sister City organizations An enthusiastic supporter of athletics, she has twice chaired "Hall of Fame" Gala events for the United States Tennis Association, Southern California Section, honoring champions of tennis. She has also led the effort to raise funds to send an equestrian participant in the sport of dressage to the United States Olympic Festival in St. Louis. Her interest in equestrian sports, tennis and her love for the outdoors motivated her support of the Land

Trust of Napa County, which serves to protect the land for current and future generations.

For several years she enjoyed being a member of the World Affairs Council; as a visionary and enthusiastic member of the Board of Governors of City of Hope Hospital she received accolades for single-handedly brokering the affiliation between City of Hope Hospital and the Los Angeles Diplomatic Corps.

In June of 2008 Mrs. Bloomberg was invited by the Ministry of Azerbaijan to participate as a keynote speaker at the international forum "Expanding the Role of Women in Cross-Cultural Dialogue," which was held in Baku, Azerbaijan. The forum was hosted in partnership by the Heydar Alivey Foundation, the First Lady of Azerbaijan, UNESCO and ISESCO. The forum brought together First Ladies of several countries and nearly four hundred luminaries and dignitaries from around the globe. In addition to her many interests, Mrs. Bloomberg continues to devote time to family and to promote culture and commerce with ongoing speaking engagements and via the print media. Together with her family, Mrs. Bloomberg, a native of Berlin and Munich, Germany, has resided in Beverly Hills and West Los Angeles for nearly fifty years. She currently divides her time between living in California and enjoying her friends in Kansas City and Washington, D.C. Connect with Mrs. Bloomberg at www.CulturalAmbassador.com.

Christina Stephens

Pauses in the Process

W hat is the path to living a successful and fulfilling life? It begins with focusing on being a giver. And in order to experience that, you have to know who you are and be true to yourself.

We are all uniquely gifted with a talent that is key to our contribution and giving our best. You can't really give your best to others if you are not true to yourself and you can't be true to yourself if you don't know who you are. When we consciously give of our best selves, we are then positioned to receive the best in return. In this way, success and fulfillment depend on giving of our most authentic selves.

Ask yourself, "Who am I? And how am I giving that to the world?" More than a decade ago, I asked myself the same question. Not long after the tragic events of 9/11, I went through a dark period when I questioned my purpose and the impact of my service. New York City is my home, and the city was in shock and mourning. At the time, I worked in a jail with adolescents who I felt I could not help in the ways they seemed to need most. Although I made a difference in the lives of many students as a teacher, there were many other students I could not help.

My mother had also recently passed away, and as I walked the streets of my brave and beautiful city, I felt the loss so deeply. I was lost, helpless, and angry at the constraints of my employment. I thought, *I'm not sure if I want to do this anymore.*

During this difficult time of uncertainty, several of the young men I was working with in the jail asked me why I had been led to such a setting. Then they said something I will never forget: "You are a sounding board for us. You give us hope. And when you forget that, another kid will come along to remind you."

Over the years I've had the privilege of running into former students who expressed gratitude for how I helped them or inspired them. I would encounter a kid, all grown up and in college, or working, but in this job, the children were not free to go about

---

I was lost, helpless, and angry at the constraints of my employment.

---

their lives. They had made mistakes and they had to pay for them. Some were innocent. But none of them could leave.

What those boys gave me that day many years ago humbled me. I went home that night and prayed. I apologized to God for complaining about my life and for being so ungrateful. I gave thanks that we had not died during the aftermath of 9/11, as I had thought we might, and I vowed to never again complain about my work as a teacher. I prayed, "I recommit to do all that I can, even in limited surroundings teaching in a prison. I vow to give my best to life at this time, in this setting, and I surrender totally to the role that my soul's path attracted during this stage of my life."

Even now, as I recall this story, I feel many emotions. I am grateful that the rich opportunities to serve, to love and to grow were mine, even when I could not fully appreciate them. I now understand that fulfilling one's purpose is a continual process and that it may or may not involve doing just one thing, or fulfilling one primary role in one's professional life. It involves what I call "pauses in the process," when life feels overwhelming, bewildering or even stagnant.

A pause in the process may mean that your heart is being made ready for your next task or being given time to absorb the love that is flowing from you and onto you. Even during these periods, we are still moving forward. Even when we feel lost, or wonder if we are making any difference at all, we are still moving forward.

I have often felt frustrated, uncertain and unappreciated by those I've worked with. These moments were just pauses in *my* process. However, as I recall my years of enriching lives through facilitating intellectual growth and life/purpose alignment coaching, I have mostly memories of joy, excitement, dedication, compassion, passion and commitment. I feel honored to know in my heart that I do work that has integrity, honor, service and love

*We ultimately encounter those
we are meant to serve.*

at its core. And, despite whatever political, economic or similar trends have come and gone, my part has been meaningful and I have made a difference.

My heart sings each time I encounter a person I have worked with in the past. It still comes as a delightful surprise to see someone who knows me as a teacher or coach. We greet or embrace each other with a smile and genuine joy. I know then, that, however long ago, I did something well. I gave each of these people my best, and they have come back to remind me.

If you are experiencing a pause in your process, know that you are still moving forward. Whatever events come into your life, there are threads that lead back to your inherent sense of calling or purpose. If your calling has been delayed or ignored during your early career, it may surface as a longing. Or you may rediscover your purpose through personal development and education. Fulfilling your purpose and giving your best, as well as receiving the best from life, has to do with the idea that we are here to contribute. To give your best, you must continually learn, discover more of whom you truly are and commit to being true to this essential self.

In doing so, your true essence and your true reason for being will be revealed.

I believe that this is a process, and yet it is the intention, the commitment to know, to honor, to live with this mission as the overriding goal in all that we choose for ourselves and in our interaction with others. Thus, we ultimately encounter those we are meant to serve.

When we accept those opportunities that allow us to offer our gifts in ways that allow us to fulfill our life's mission, we give our best to life. At any stage along the way, we may, for various reasons, settle or give in to fear, insecurity, unpreparedness, limited awareness or other false or limiting beliefs. Ideas accepted from

Take time to journal key life experiences.

the thoughts of others may hinder what this "best" will be or the level of contribution we are able to make.

However, if our heart's desire and intent is to have giving as a dominating theme in our life's philosophy, there is a design in life that supports this both in outpouring and in the generosity of the universe (God's delivery system) returning to us. These are not new thoughts, but I believe them to be true and I have seen this principle at work in my life as well as in the lives of others. I believe that to live with giving as a vital and essential approach to life will lead us down the path to experiencing success from the heart.

Each person is unique, with a unique set of abilities that shall be discovered, explored and developed as a part of our spiritual blueprint. That blueprint shows the purpose each one of is intended to fulfill. I believe this purpose is a choice that can be pursued through varied pathways, and can manifest in different ways—including the pauses in the process.

Much will be revealed in the interruptions of life, the changes and challenges, the detours and delays. To understand the true meaning of the pauses in your process, take time to journal key life experiences, both personal and professional. Reflect on these events and assess how they contributed to your understanding of yourself. What value did these experiences have? How did they help you contribute to others? Who benefited, and, if it was an unexpected benefit, what did you learn? List ten things you have done to help others.

My work as a teacher has given me a great variety of opportunities to make meaningful contributions—to give my students my best. Teaching has been a channel to foster the development of the best in me as I've made my contributions to others. I have flourished not only in my role as a teacher and a mentor, but also as a coach and conscious seeker of truth. Despite past frustrations and challenges and through all of the pauses in my process, I can say with heartfelt sincerity that teaching embodies the essence of my purpose: to teach, to inspire, to guide, to learn and, through these actions, to love.

I once had the privilege of seeing my heart beating. I was in awe, and as I think of that image now, I am reminded that the most precious gift we are continually being given is the gift of life. When I am tempted to grow weary, or become distracted by the variety of life in process, I remember my overall purpose: "to give my best to life" and I pick myself up and get to the work of living and giving my best, authentic self to the world.

Christina Stephens is the founder of Defining the Future You, which uses soul-centered practices to guide individuals in their journey to discover their true callings and to balanced and fulfilling lives. The mission of Defining the Future You is to connect people to the core life values of love, gratitude and service.

A lifestyle and empowerment coach, teacher, mentor and speaker, Christina has worked both nationally and internationally with individuals and groups from all walks of life. In truth and with compassion, she speaks with the intention of assisting others to live from their hearts with gratitude, authenticity and in a spirit of service. Connect with Christina at www.DefiningTheFutureYou.com.

3-Day **REIGNITE** Weekend
SEMINAR VOUCHER

As a reward for taking the first step toward transforming your business and life, by following your heart, Adam Markel and New Peaks is offering you and one guest an exclusive opportunity to attend the 3-Day REIGNITE Weekend Seminar as VIPs.

At this world famous program, you will uncover your inner-fire for success and kick-start your purpose, power and game plan for creating even more fulfillment and inner peace, both personally and professionally.

You will change your life forever!

To redeem your Seminar Voucher and register, visit www.ReigniteWeekend.com or call 1-888-868-8883, option 2

When registering, please use
PROMO Code: HEART-SUCCESS

NEW PEAKS™
TRANSFORMATION THROUGH EDUCATION

Adam Markel
CEO, New Peaks

*This offer is open to all purchasers of *Success from the Heart* by Adam Markel. Limit one Voucher per copy of *Success from the Heart* by Adam Markel. Voucher may only be applied to the **3-Day REIGNITE Weekend** and is not redeemable for cash or other New Peaks seminars. Seminar registration is subject to availability and/or changes to program schedule.

SPECIAL BONUS OFFER

Exclusive Scholarship for New Peaks 3-Day REIGNITE Weekend.

You are being invited to attend our LIVE New Peaks 3-Day REIGNITE Weekend program where you can deepen your focus, passion and purpose. You will receive 2 VIP tickets, so you can share this powerful experience with a loved one or business associate.

This is a course that will transform your life and reignite your fire for creating a life filled with inner peace, passion and love.

At the 3-Day REIGNITE Weekend, you will expand upon the teachings in this book, as well as dive deeper into:

- Learning your heart virtues.
- Creating your success formula.
- Money and wealth reconditioning.
- How to create an unstoppable team.
- 7 pillars to an incredible relationship.
- The ultimate code of conduct and HOW to use it.
- The 2 questions that distinguish a 10X business thinker.

- Business and branding strategy.
- High-level masterminding.
- Creating powerful rituals.
- Creating your action steps.

Plus:

- Learning your heart virtues.
- Business Real Estate Training.
- Breakthrough Networking Session.
- Stock Training.
- And more!

After graduating REIGNITE, you will have the tools to break free from any limiting beliefs that are holding you back and take action toward living a life that you absolutely LOVE. You'll have specific strategies to create even greater success in your business and relationships, as well as tools to help you stay focused and on-purpose.

To find out more about REIGNITE and to secure your spot to this transformational event, please visit www.ReigniteWeekend.com and enter promo code HEART-SUCCESS to redeem your VIP TICKETS, or call 1-888-868-8883 x 2.

Your Complimentary gift is for 2 VIP Tickets to REIGNITE, a 3-day weekend that will guide you through reigniting your passion, purpose and drive for greater success.